The
Legal Principles
of
Medical Practice

EXPLAINED

Deborah J. Wear-Finkle, MD, MPA

Rapid Psychler Press ♂♀

Suite 374   Suite 203
3560 Pine Grove Ave.   1673 Richmond St.
Port Huron, Michigan   London, Ontario
USA 48060   **Canada** N6G 2N3

Toll Free Phone   888-PSY-CHLE (888-779-2453)
Toll Free Fax   888-PSY-CHLR (888-779-2457)
Outside the U.S. & Canada — Phone 519-667-2335
Outside the U.S. & Canada — Fax 519-675-0610
website   www.psychler.com
email   rapid@psychler.com

ISBN 1-894328-27-2
© 2003, Rapid Psychler Press — First Edition, First Printing
Printed in the United States of America

All caricatures are fictitious. Any resemblance to real people, either living or deceased, is entirely coincidental. The author assumes no responsibility for any medical, legal, or ethical decisions made on the basis of the contents of this book. Such determinations should be made after consultation with the appropriate physician, lawyer, or ethics committee member, respectively. Every effort was made to ensure the information provided in this book was accurate at the time of publication. However, due to the rapidly changing medicolegal field, the reader is encouraged to consult additional sources of information.

Dedication

To my son, Kyle.

The wonder, simple wisdom, and love of a child are what make everything else in life possible and worthwhile.

To the crew of the Columbia — each of whom personify the total commitment to a dream and to a goal much greater than ourselves.

Acknowledgments

- Harold Bursztajn, M.D. — without whose support the original book would not have been possible, and who helped me believe I had something valuable to contribute

- Thomas Gutheil, M.D. — whose brilliant teaching first sparked a love of law and ethics in medical practice, as it has for countless others, and continues to be a strong motivating force

- My friend and colleague, Terry Riley, M.D. — whose wit, intellect, friendship, and unflagging support are deeply appreciated

- David J. Robinson, M.D. — who makes the business of authoring/publishing seem simple and painless

- Brian Chapman — whose illustrations are absolutely brilliant and help break the monotony of the subject matter while giving it soul

- My loving family who give 100% support to all my endeavors

Introduction

In mid 2000, the hardcover text called *Medicolegal Issues in Clinical Practice, A Primer for the Legally Challenged* was released. This book received very positive reviews along with many requests for a condensed version. The majority of physicians have precious little time for lengthy discussions about legal issues, but do want to understand basic medicolegal principles. This condensed version has been updated to include many of the changes that have taken place in the medicolegal realm since 2000.

I hope to convey one clear message. If you understand and practice *ethical* medicine, you will be on a good footing *legally*. Ethical standards are usually set at a slightly higher bar than legal requirements.

Knowledge is indeed power. Whether you are practicing in a state with a malpractice insurance crisis or one with adequate tort reform, chances are that you did not learn all you needed to know in medical school (or kindergarten, for that matter).

This book offers you the chance to minimize your liability by learning about the basics of law as it commonly affects physicians and medical practices.

D.J.W.-F.
Brunswick, ME
March, 2003

Table of Contents

Chapter 1 — Introduction to Legal Principles   **7**
1.1   The Relationship Between Ethics and Law   7
1.2   History of Medical Ethics   7
1.3   The Scope of Malpractice Litigation   9
1.4   Why Do Patients Sue?   11

Chapter 2 — Legal Stuff   **14**
2.1   Criminal, Civil, and Administrative Law   14
2.2   Sources of Law   14
2.3   Medical Malpractice Law/Torts 101   16
2.4   The Four Arms of Any Negligence Case   16
2.5   Standard of Care   20
2.6   Medical Malpractice Litigation Process   24
2.7   Different States, Different Rules   25
2.8   Res Ipsa Loquitor   26
2.9   Vicarious Liability   27
2.10   Respondeat Superior   28
2.11   National Practitioner Data Bank   29
2.12   Clinical Practice Guidelines   29
2.13   Nuisance Lawsuits   30
2.14   Intentional Torts   30
2.15   Regulatory Stuff   34
2.16   Anti-Conflict of Interest Laws   39
2.17   State Regulatory Agencies   41
2.18   EMTALA   42
2.19   Americans with Disabilities Act   44
2.20   Occupation, Safety, and Health Administration   46
2.21   Equal Opportunity Commission   47
2.22   Professional Liability Insurance   48

Chapter 3 — Doctor-Patient Relationships and Clinical Issues
    50
3.1   Informed Consent   50
3.2   Competence/Capacity to Make Medical Decisions   59
3.3   Research   65

3.4	Minors	66
3.5	The Right to Refuse Treatment	68
3.6	Leaving Hospital Against Medical Advice	69
3.7	False Imprisonment	71
3.8	Confidentiality	72
3.9	Exceptions to the Confidentiality of Medical Information	74
3.10	End of Life Issues	81
3.11	Physician-Assisted Suicide	85
3.12	Ethics Committees	86
3.13	Hospice	87
3.14	Boundary Issues	88
3.15	Standby	93
3.16	Dual Relationships with Patients	94
3.17	Abandonment	94
3.19	Good Samaritan Laws	96

Chapter 4 — Odds and Ends — **100**

4.1	Prescribing Issues	100
4.2	Conflicts of Interest	105
4.3	Technology	108
4.4	Oops!	109

Chapter 5 — Limiting Liability — **112**

5.1	Patient Safety	112
5.2	Communication	113
5.3	Patients Who Have Chronic Diseases	114
5.4	Documentation	115
5.5	Corrections to Medical Records	116
5.6	Consultations	120
5.7	Process Issues	122

22 Commandments for a Legally Sound Practice — **124**

Index — **126**

About the Author and Artist — **128**

1. Introduction to Legal Principles

1.1 – The Relationship between Ethics and Law

Ethics, a branch of philosophy, pertains to the *principles* of proper or morally correct conduct within a society. **Law** defines the *rules* of conduct that have been established by a society.

The relationship between ethics and law is as follows — basic ethical principles frequently lead to the development of law through case precedent and statute. The relationship between the two is dynamic and based on many forces in society, the nation, and the world.

Initially, a focus develops on an issue within a society. If enough people feel strongly about the moral "rightness" of the subject, a significant power base develops and legislation may follow. In this way, legislation formalizes the rules governing certain behaviors.

Even laws are not sufficient to bind individuals to abide by ethical principles. Some regulatory bodies set their standards at an *ethical*, as opposed to *legal*, level. Those to whom the regulations apply must then follow the stated standards. An example of this principle involves state boards of medicine. These boards, after full and fair hearings, may suspend or revoke the licenses of physicians even if a law hasn't been broken. In other instances, court decisions set precedents based on the ethical issues involved in the dispute. Some of the more common non-medical issues involve: abortion rights, capital punishment, and civil commitment. There is no doubt that the majority of physicians are unequivocally committed to the ethical practice of medicine. **Medical ethics** focuses on doing what is considered morally right in the evaluation and treatment of patients.

1.2 – History of Medical Ethics

Medical ethics has a long history, beginning with the **Oath of Hippocrates**, which is really a concise statement of principles. The Oath was created during the period of Greek prosperity around the 5th

Century BC. While the Oath was adapted in the 10th or 11th Century AD to eliminate references to paganism, it remains the quintessential statement of ideal conduct for physicians, and the ideal in stating patients' rights. The two primary principles of medical ethics are:

Autonomy — the right of every competent person to be able to decide what will be done medically to him or her.

Beneficence — meaning "do good for the patient," also known as **nonmalfeasance,** or "do no harm."

Thomas Percival, an English physician, made a significant contribution to Western medical ethics with the publication of his Code of Medical Ethics in 1803. In 1847, the first official meeting of the **American Medical Association (AMA)** was held. At that meeting, the founding members adopted the first American Code of Ethics, which was based on Percival's code. Although there have been revisions, the essence of this code has been maintained and is available at **www.ama-assn.org**

Ethical values and legal principles are often closely related, *but ethical obligations typically exceed legal duties.* Being cleared of any legal wrongdoing does not necessarily clear charges of unethical conduct within a professional society or board of medicine. Physicians who belong to one or more national medical groups are sent statements of ethics developed by such specialty or subspecialty societies. Membership to these organizations indicates a commitment to the ethical principles so espoused. If a member is charged with violating an ethical principle, the appropriate committee within the organization conducts an investigation. If the charge is found to be valid, the member may be sanctioned or expelled. When this occurs, it may be publicized, and the action sent to that member's state of licensure. It behooves you to be aware of the stated ethical principles of the societies to which you belong.

☞ Caveat

Ensuring the autonomy of your patients always enhances your ethical and legal standing. Not doing so puts you in jeopardy.

1.3 — The Scope of Malpractice Litigation

We all know that we are in the midst of a national medical malpractice insurance crisis. There may soon be federal legislation to address the skyrocketing premiums. As a physician, you have approximately a 50% chance of being named in a lawsuit in your practice lifetime (this also depends on your specialty and style of practice). Because of this, you need to know how to minimize your risks and liabilities. The scope and extent of medical malpractice litigation is quite broad, but it could be much worse. Here are some factoids to consider:

A. Between 1977–1992 there were 12,829 physicians involved in 8,231 closed claims, an analysis of which reveals that:
* Physician care was defensible in 62% of cases and indefensible in 25% (the remainder were indeterminate)
* The plaintiff received payment in 43% of the overall number of claims; patients still received money in 21% of cases where medical care could be defended, but did not always receive money (91%) in cases where medical care could not be defended
* The severity of the injury was not associated with the payment rate in cases resolved by a jury; other studies have revealed that the severity of the disability predicts an award for the plaintiff (not simply that an adverse event occurred, or that there was negligence involved)

B. In an annual report to Congress in 1991, the Physician Payment Review Commission noted that awards were higher (using identical juries) when it seemed that the defendant could pay more. Jury awards for leg amputation cases (in various scenarios) were:
* $199,999 — auto accident case
* $330,000 — private property owner case
* $687,000 — product liability case
* $754,000 — medical malpractice against a physician
* $761,000 — worker's compensation

C. There has been a definite and continued increase in the amount of money awarded in medical malpractice cases. For example, from 1995 to 1998 in North Florida:

- The size of the *average* plaintiff verdict has increased from $1.2 million (1995) to $2.6 million (1998)
- The size of the *median* award rose from $270,000 to $665,000
- This compares (favorably?!) with the 1998 *average* award in New York City of $6.1 million, and a *median* of $1.1 million!

(Author's Note: Sincere apologies to those who have provided data from good and valid research. When addressing medical malpractice, there is a huge body of contradictory data, which is why I prefer to call them "factoids" in this book.)

Now to the "glass is half full" part. There have been several excellent studies looking at hospital admissions and outcomes from the 1970's through the 1990's. One very consistent finding is that 1% of all hospital records reveal that an injury was caused by negligence, yet less than 10% of these injuries lead to a formal claim.

Other factoids:
- Less than 10% of all lawsuits go to juries, and of these, two-thirds find in favor of the defendant physicians (even when physician peer-reviewers found the level of care indefensible half of the time!)
- Approximately 4% of all hospitalizations result in adverse events, and more than one-quarter of these are due to substandard care
- There is a 12-fold variation in the rates of adverse events between facilities and physicians; the percentage due to negligence ranges from 0 to 70%
- It is estimated that there are 180,000 deaths annually that can be attributed to iatrogenic causes; half of these are due to negligence

Since 2000, the size of some awards have continued to grow, and several states are in the midst of a crisis. Many physicians, unable to afford their malpractice insurance premiums, are limiting their practices. The direction that we as physicians should take is to minimize variation in practice, the incidence of avoidable adverse events, and in particular, the numbers of injuries and deaths due to negligence. In spite of all the negative information you hear, remember that only 10% of cases ever get to a jury trial, and of this 10%, about two-thirds of juries find in favor of the defendant physician(s).

1.4 — Why Do Patients Sue?

Before launching into an overview of negligence, consider this simple equation:

Medical Malpractice Suit = Bad Outcome + Bad Feelings

A bad outcome is just that — there *must* be some tangible physical or psychological injury. Although a patient may not like a physician's appearance or demeanor, or not improve from the treatment provided, these are not adequate grounds for a lawsuit. The point is that there must be an actual *injury* (more on this to follow).

We all know physicians who are not top notch in the skills department and who do at times have bad outcomes. Yet, their patients never seem to sue. Why? *Because their patients like them.* These physicians probably have great interpersonal skills and demonstrate genuine concern. Active listening, interested facial expressions and demeanor all indicate empathy. As far as patients are concerned, these doctors can do no wrong (which emphasizes the importance of peer review in some cases). At the other end of the spectrum, we have some colleagues about whom you might joke, "I would never see Dr. I.M. Godsgift unless I was *really* sick." These are the folks who may be brilliant in their particular fields, but have almost reptilian personalities. They usually don't see this as a problem, or may be so arrogant they don't care. But the patients and their families do. In many lawsuits, the issue of effective communication is a major theme. Speaking to a person using polysyllabic jargon and in a condescending manner does not constitute effective communication. The resentment that most people feel when they are spoken down to may not become evident if everything goes well. When there is a problem, however, the resentment bubbles to the surface and finds somewhere to vent (like a bad remake of *Poltergeist*).

Many authors report a quasi-rule of thirds:
- One-third of patients will never sue
- One-third will sue if they ever get a chance
- One-thire fall somewhere between

Be wary of the last group and don't give them a reason to seek out an attorney with your name on a subpoena.

One survey found that 98% of patients wanted or expected their doctor to acknowledge an error, even if it caused no harm. The patients who suffered from moderate-to-severe errors were more likely to report the doctor to various authorities or consider suing if the doctor failed to disclose errors. Most people do not expect their doctors to be perfect, but they do expect them to be honest. A study of families who sued their child's doctor after a perinatal injury showed that 24% of those who filed a lawsuit did so when they realized the physician:
- Was not completely honest
- Allowed them to believe things that were not true
- Intentionally mislead them

Another 20% sued because they said it was the only way they could find out what really happened! One unsettling editorial by a physician spoke of his recommendation to a friend that he sue his surgeon after an operation that removed all but the upper 5% of his stomach. What was initially thought to be gastric cancer turned out to be peptic ulcer disease. What angered the patient (and his physician friend) was the flippant response of the surgeon who offered neither an explanation nor an apology.

☞ **Caveat**
Do the right thing for the right patient, do it in the right way, and do it safely.

References

American Medical Association: **Code of Medical Ethics – Current Opinions with Annotations.**
American Medical Association, Chicago, 2002.

Borbjerg RR: **Medical Malpractice and Folklore, Facts, and the Future.**
Annals of Int Med 117:788-791, 1992

Bozeman FC: **Sky-High South Florida Verdicts Spread to North Florida.**
Escambia County Medical Society Bulletin, Oct 1999

Brennan T: **The Harvard Medical Practice Study.** *The Mental Health Practitioner and the Law.*
Harvard University Press, Cambridge, 1998

Brennan TA, Sox CM, Burstin HR: **Relation Between Negligent Adverse Events in the Outcomes of Medical Malpractice Litigation.**
N Engl J Med 335:1963-1967, 1996

Crane M: **Malpractice Wars.**
Medical Economics 26, July 1999

Hickson GB, Clayton EW, Githens PB, et al: **Factors That Prompted Families to File Medical Malpractice Claims Following Perinatal Injuries.**
JAMA 267:1359-1363, 1992

Lally JJ: **Why I Urged My Friend to Sue His Doctors.**
Medical Economics 151-152, July 26, 1999

Sloan FA: **Medical Malpractice Experience of Physicians: Predictable Or Haphazard?**
JAMA 262:3291, 1989

Taragin MI, Willett LR, Wilcek AP et al: **The Influence of Standard Of Care and Severity of Injury on the Resolution of Medical Malpractice Claims.**
Annals of Int Med 117:780-784, 1992

Vidmar N: *Medical Malpractice and the American Jury.*
University of Michigan Press, Ann Arbor, 1997

Witman AB, Park DM, Hardin SB: **How Do Patients Want Physicians to Handle Mistakes?**
Arch Intern Med 156:2565-2569, 1996

2. Legal Stuff

2.1 – Criminal, Civil, and Administrative Law

There are three principal types of law in the U.S. — criminal, civil, and administrative. The basis of U.S. law is derived from our Constitution and from English common law. The goal of **criminal law** is to effect justice and to dispense punishment for crimes committed. The aim of **civil law** is to make restitution to the wronged party, or "to make whole again." The roots of this tradition go back to the Talmud. Today, the "making whole" usually has to do with $$$. **Administrative law** refers to the regulatory processes developed by administrative bodies. There may be criminal or civil suits that result from actions stemming from administrative law.

2.2 – Sources of Law

2.2.1 – The United States Constitution

The constitution established the U.S. as a republic and provided the structure of our system of congress. It is the gold standard by which all other laws applied to Americans are judged. In addition to the Articles, it also includes the Bill of Rights.

2.2.2 – Bill of Rights

The Bill of Rights further defines the individual rights of American citizens. Interestingly, several states would not ratify the Constitution without a guarantee that individual rights would be protected. Some of these rights are: freedom of speech, freedom of the press, freedom of religion, freedom to assemble and protest, protection against unreasonable searches and seizures of property, protection against cruel and unusual punishment, etc. The majority of the 16 additional amendments expand individual rights and freedoms.

2.2.3 – State Constitutions

Every state has its own constitution and laws. The only guiding principle is that state laws cannot conflict with federal law. They can be more comprehensive in the protection of individual rights than federal laws, but not less so. For example, federal law amended the **standard of**

proof for civil commitment to be that of "clear and convincing evidence." States with lesser standards (i.e. preponderance of evidence), were then required to adopt the federal standard. States already requiring the higher standard were free to keep it. The goal of this implementation was to protect every individual's right to freedom, and if an error occurred, it was in the direction of enhancing liberty.

2.2.4 – Statutes

Statutes are laws adopted by elected officials and by the U.S. Congress. Some of the statutes that are important for healthcare practitioners are the: **Occupational Safety and Health Act (OSHA)**, **Americans with Disabilities Act (ADA)**, **Civil Rights Act (CRA)**, **False Claims Act (FCA)**, and the **Food and Drug Act**.

2.2.5 – Regulatory or Administrative Law

For many, the regulations enacted by numerous local, state, and federal agencies have a more pervasive impact on daily life than many of the more prominent sources listed above. Examples of administrative agencies that affect healthcare workers are: **Occupational Safety and Health Administration**, **Food and Drug Administration (FDA)**, **Equal Employment Opportunity Commission (EEOC)**, **Department of Health and Human Services,** and the **National Labor Relations Board (NLRB)**. For healthcare professionals requiring licensure, state licensing boards are also very powerful regulatory agencies.

2.2.6 – Common Law

Common law dates back to 12th century England. When there were no legal precedents to assist judges, they applied current customs and common sense to arrive at a decision.

2.2.7 – Case Law

This is also known as "judge-made law." Case law develops when judges interpret and apply sources of law in particular cases. A decision so rendered then sets a precedent for future cases in that jurisdiction, as well as in similar and lower courts. Decisions made by the U.S. Supreme Court provide a precedent for all other similar cases in the country. **Stare decisis** (Latin for "let the decision stand") means that controlling case law can only be modified by a higher-level court. Only the Supreme Court can modify one of its own decisions, and this rarely happens. Medical negligence cases are almost always determined by case law.

2.3 – Medical Malpractice Law/Torts 101

As any first year law student will tell you, one of the most boring yet crucial courses is *Introduction to Tort Law*. A **tort** is any civil wrong against another person. Tort law covers civil actions between two parties, defined as either intentional or unintentional torts. **Intentional torts** are deliberate actions that may cause damage. They are not usually covered by malpractice insurance. Examples include: assault and battery, sexual relationships with patients, and false imprisonment. **Unintentional torts** are actions that possess an unreasonable risk of causing harm. Medical malpractice falls under this area of negligence law.

2.4 – The Four Arms of Any Negligence Case

2.4.1 – The 4 D's

There are four components required for a negligence action to be considered valid. These are called the four D's of negligence (similar to the four F's of gallbladder disease). The four D's that a plaintiff must establish for a successful negligence suit are:

- **Duty** (of a doctor to a patient)
- **Dereliction** of duty, or a deviation from the standard of care
- **Direct causation** of the problem
- **Damage** (an injury was caused)

For a negligence suit to be considered by the courts (or, as the lawyers say "have merit"), some form of injury — physical or emotional — must have occurred. If not, a lawsuit cannot be launched, even if a physician has blatantly violated accepted standards of care. On the other hand, an unfavorable outcome for one of your patients does not mean you will automatically be sued. Depending on your specialty and the acuity level of your patients, there is the ever-present risk of unfavorable outcomes. When they occur, it does not reflect on you as a physician. Uncertainty, illness, and yes, death, are integral parts of medical practice. Neurosurgeons, for example, understand that a large percentage of their patients are expected to fare poorly. Psychiatrists, at some point during their careers, can expect at least one patient to commit suicide.

To begin a negligence case, duty must first be established. A **duty** to a patient begins any time there is a **doctor-patient relationship**. When a doctor-patient relationship is established, the doctor has a responsibility to provide a certain **standard of care** (**SOC**) for that patient. If there is evidence that the SOC isn't upheld, a **dereliction of the duty** is considered to have occurred, which is the next link necessary in a successful malpractice action. The final step involves demonstrating that the dereliction (or deviation from the SOC) was the **direct causation** of the patient's injury (**damage**).

2.4.2 – Standard of Proof

Each of the four elements in alleged negligence cases must be proven to a specific legal standard. If you have ever testified as an expert witness or read a case transcript, you will be familiar with the following statement made by expert witnesses, *"I can state with reasonable medical certainty that. . ."*

The legal standard of proof required in negligence cases in almost all jurisdictions is called a **preponderance of evidence**. This is considered to be "more likely than not" or, for those who think numerically, at least 51% certainty. With few exceptions, the plaintiff in a malpractice claim must show, with a *preponderance of evidence*, that the alleged negligence was indeed the defendant's responsibility. This is the legal standard used in most civil cases.

Other legal standards exist. The next highest standard of proof is called that of **clear and convincing evidence**. This is used in civil cases where there is a more substantial right at risk (rather than mere monetary remuneration), such as someone's liberty (as in a civil commitment), or the right of a hospitalized psychiatric patient to refuse medication. The clear and convincing standard is considered to be somewhere in the vicinity of 75 to 85% certainty.

The highest standard of proof is called **beyond a reasonable doubt**, and is considered to be about 95% certainty. This standard is applied in criminal cases where the defendant's liberty or life is at risk, and in some jurisdictions for specific civil actions. To believe something beyond a reasonable doubt means "you better be darn sure!"

2.4.3 – Duty

Duty to a patient is established by formally providing medical services, such as assignment to your primary care panel or in a consultation. It can also be implied, as in working in an emergency room (ER) and treating patients seeking care there. Situations that are less clear might involve a neighbor requesting your medical advice. The law presumes that when a physician provides some form of evaluation/treatment, even informally, a duty to that person has been established. You may want to rethink the "cocktail party consult" the next time you are asked for your advice — or at least be very circumspect in your comments. It is safe to say something like *"That's a good question — I think you should contact your doctor about this matter as it is not really appropriate for me to give you advice."* Once a doctor-patient relationship has been established, the physician has the duty to provide treatment for that person at the established standard of care.

2.4.4 – Direct Causation

Determining cause in malpractice cases generally involves two factors:
• **Cause-in-fact**, which refers to whether or not the injury would have occurred "but for" the doctor's actions
• **Proximate cause**, which is a substantial factor in the resultant injury; this also is related to the concept of **foreseeability**

Legal and medical perspectives differ on how an action is seen as the direct cause of an injury. In medicine, we are used to diagnosing a disease and determining the causative agent, which (frequently) becomes the focus of treatment. From a legal standpoint, direct or proximate cause is determined by looking at whether the action *foreseeably* could have caused the injury, and whether the injury would not have occurred "but for" the actions of the physician.

2.4.5 – Damage

Any successful medical malpractice lawsuit must contain evidence that some type of injury was sustained. Such "damage" is usually a compensable injury or a death that occurs because of a specific act or omission. The most common types of acts or omissions include:

- Incorrect diagnosis
- Delays in making a diagnosis or instituting treatment
- Providing inappropriate treatment
- Medication side-effects or errors
- Procedural errors

The type of compensation that plaintiffs seek is referred to as **damages** (not to be confused with injury), of which there are three types:

- Economic
- Non-economic
- Punitive

Economic damages are the costs that are directly associated with the injury. These can include medical bills, lost wages, and loss of earning potential.

Non-economic damages are also known as **compensatory damages**, and are moneys given for things like "pain and suffering," "loss of consortium" with a spouse, or "lost quality of life." Some jurisdictions do not allow compensation for non-economic damages without a physical or psychological injury, and some do not allow non-economic damages at all. Several states also have **caps** (an upper limit) on the total amount that can be collected for these types of damages. The current malpractice insurance crisis affecting many states, has led to requests for a reasonable cap on non-economic damages. This is initiative is presently under consideration at the federal level.

Punitive damages are awarded to the plaintiff(s) to punish the defendant. When punitive damages are awarded, the cases usually involve very clear acts of negligence. Punitive damages are rarely levied against physicians. They are much more likely to be sought in lawsuits against organizations, drug companies, etc.

An example of punitive damages involved the General Motors Corporation. In this action, economic and non-economic damages totaling $107.6 million dollars were awarded to the plaintiffs, who had experienced severe burns when their vehicles burst into flames after being rear-ended. There was an additional *$48 billion dollars* awarded in punitive damages. This case was seen as being particularly egregious by the jury because clear documentation was provided that GM management decided not to recall the automobiles with the problem (once they were aware of it) because it would cost more to fix the problem than it would to defend a lawsuit. This blatant disregard for consumer safety clearly didn't sit well with the jury.

Examples of punitive damages in the healthcare arena can be found in recent lawsuits against two large managed care organizations. The first case involves the 1998 multimillion-dollar Kentucky jury award against Humana, Inc. Here, economic damages were limited to the payment of medical bills. The remainder of the award was given for punitive damages. This case was followed by the January, 1999 verdict of $116 million against Aetna Healthplans of California.

2.5 — Standard of Care

The **standard of care** (**SOC**) is generally defined as practicing with the same reasonable level of skill that a prudent physician with similar training and experience would recognize as adequate and acceptable in similar circumstances. You are encouraged to check with your state medical practice statutes for the exact definition. With few exceptions, the SOC is based on national standards, not local ones. The definition of SOC does not necessarily specify the best, most expensive, or technologically advanced care that could be provided. Rather, it refers to care that is considered "acceptable" and "adequate" by similarly trained practitioners working under similar circumstances.

2.5.1 – How Do I Measure Standard of Care?

This is indeed the million-dollar question (pun intended). It would be great if there were absolute parameters in each case of alleged medical negligence, but this isn't so. Most definitions contain vague terms like "acceptable" and "reasonable."

Because the SOC is based on the care that a similarly trained doctor would provide, most state laws clearly indicate that not just any physician can testify as an expert witness. If the charges are against a non-residency trained general practitioner, then the doctor presenting testimony will have similar training and experience. If the alleged malpractice involves a board-certified neurosurgeon, an obstetrician would not be called to testify.

Many jurisdictions abandoned "local standards" because it was difficult to get physicians who live in the same area to testify against each other. With the improvements in communication technology, it is reasonable that physicians are held accountable to a national standard. The SOC is derived from many sources, including the **Joint Commission for the Accreditation of Healthcare Organizations (JCAHO)** standards, specialty guidelines, local facility policies, and of course, state and federal law. The SOC evolves over time, and the courts look to medical experts for guidance on these issues. This is the reason that most jurisdictions require that an expert witness in a medical malpractice case have training and experience similar to the defendant.

An example of an evolving SOC is the use of beta-blockers at the time of hospital discharge following a myocardial infarction (MI). In the early 1990's it became evident that there was significantly less morbidity and mortality in patients who were treated with beta-blockers after an MI. The American Heart Association recommended that this treatment be considered for all patients upon discharge from hospital. Over the following several years, the data collected were even more conclusive. Articles and recommendations for the use of beta-blockers were published in general medical journals and accessible to all physicians who treated patients with MIs. After several additional studies noted a continued high rate of underutilization of beta-blockers in the post-MI period, the **American Medical Association (AMA)** made a formal recommendation in late 1998. This was in the form of a Quality Care Alert mailed to all its members. The alert stated that the use of beta-blockers after an MI must at least be considered. If physicians chose not to use them, then they had to document their rationale for not doing so. This clearly established the standard of care in for post-MI treatment.

2.5.2 – Further Comments on Standard of Care

Be careful if you prescribe a medication for a non-FDA approved use. Always document your rationale, which should be supportable by peer review references. Also, the **Physicians Desk Reference (PDR)** has been used as the SOC in several cases when a drug was used in a dosage outside the recommended range, or for a different duration of treatment. You can use a drug in ways that you believe are appropriate as long as you have a supportable rationale for doing so.

Another interesting catch is that if the alleged injury is said to be caused by a deviation from the SOC, and the physician did not follow the recommendations in the PDR, the standard of proof may shift to the defense in some jurisdictions. This means that *you* must prove, with a preponderance of the evidence, that you met the SOC instead of the plaintiff needing to prove that you did not.

There are many times where it is perfectly appropriate to use a drug for a non-approved use, just be certain to note why, and on what basis (preferably with firmly rooted, current medical evidence available from peer-reviewed journals). Well-conducted, prospective, double-blind studies are required for medications to receive FDA approval. Such studies are frequently funded by pharmaceutical companies. Two key reasons that a drug company may not be particularly interested in pursuing FDA approval (and committing millions of dollars to research) are:

- Where the group of persons who might benefit from that particular use of the drug would be small and provide a scant return on the financial investment, or
- When the patent for a particular drug is due to expire in the near future

2.5.3 – Alternative Treatments and Standard of Care

A brief introduction is provided here on alternative/complementary medicine and SOC. Alternative treatments include therapies ranging from herbal medicines to acupuncture. Rather than debating the merits of such treatments, a caution will be given: *If there is evidence that you prescribed an alternative treatment that allegedly led to an injury, you will not have met the SOC if other prudent, similarly trained and experienced physicians would not also consider this treatment in a similar situation.*

☞ **Caveat**

Familiarize yourself with all the policies that your organization has in place, as well as the guidelines your practice has developed. All local policies will be used as legal evidence to establish the SOC under which you should be practicing. Facility/organization policies should state the minimum standards required by law (and not set a higher standard). The same goes for JCAHO/**National Committee of Quality Assurance** (**NCQA**) standards. Even if your organization is not accredited by either organization, meeting the basic standards set by these organizations is a good idea and demonstrates a commitment to providing quality care. If you practice in a JCAHO or NCQA accredited institution, these standards will be considered to be the SOC for your organization.

2.6 – Medical Malpractice Litigation Process

There are many steps involved in a medical malpractice lawsuit, and the process varies from state to state. An example of the preliminary process (prior to the actual trial) in Florida is as follows:

1. A dissatisfied patient/family speaks with a lawyer to discuss legal action. The impetus for a lawsuit may have come from speaking with others, a decision following a period of personal reflection, or after mounting frustration at the lack of information after a bad outcome.

2. The patient or family, called the **plaintiff(s)**, must have a lawyer perform a pre-suit investigation of all factors involved in the claim. Written corroboration from a medical expert witness stating that there are reasonable grounds to support the claim of negligence is necessary.

3. At this point, the plaintiff's lawyer can provide a notice of intent to submit a claim against the defendants listed (in the "deep pockets" theory of litigation all potential parties are named, see Section 2.9).

4. The defense then conducts an investigation to determine if the defendants were negligent in the care or treatment of the plaintiff to the point of causing an injury. If this is not found to be the case, such a finding requires a written expert statement from a physician who has training and experience similar to that of the defendant.

5. Following the pre-suit investigation, any party can file a motion to request that the court (judge) determine if pursuing the claim is reasonable or not.

6. The parties may elect to have damages awarded by **arbitration**, which is one of two forms of **alternative dispute resolution** (**ADR**). **Mediation** is the other. Punitive damages cannot be awarded in ADR.

7. Upon receipt of a claim, the prospective defendant(s) can make an offer to admit liability and accept arbitration, which must be made within 50 days. If arbitration is rejected, a lawsuit may be filed within 60 days, or before the statute of limitations (see below).

8. If a settlement is accepted, the parties have 30 days to agree on an amount. If this is not achievable, the case goes to binding arbitration.

Though convoluted, this sequence of events provides opportunities for minimizing the number of cases that proceed to trial, while ensuring that individuals are able to receive fair compensation for their injuries.

2.7 – Different States, Different Rules

A comparison of different states reveals wide variation between jurisdictions. You can review the laws that govern your state by checking the website **http://www.mcandl.com**, which has a summary of each state's medical malpractice laws. Some key areas are:

2.7.1 – Statute of Limitations

A **statute of limitations** (**SOL**) is the amount of time a plaintiff has to file a lawsuit following the injury. Different states have different SOLs, and they vary considerably. The SOL can also vary if there is evidence of fraud or an attempt to conceal mistakes. The period of time a plaintiff has to initiate a claim may be extended in such cases. If the family is suing for a wrongful death action (as a result of malpractice), then a different set of rules apply.

2.7.2 – Contributory Negligence

Contributory negligence is the consideration as to whether the plaintiff contributed to the injury that is the focus of the lawsuit. This frequently becomes an issue when a patient is noncompliant with treatment or does not take responsibility for maintaining a healthy life style.

2.7.3 – Vicarious Liability

This is a consideration of whether any additional person or organization, by virtue of their relationship to the defendant, also has responsibility for injury to the plaintiff (this is also presented below).

2.7.4 –Expert Testimony

Expert testimony may be a required step in filing a lawsuit. Increasingly, affidavits are required at the time of filing (or shortly afterwards), which assert the validity of the allegations made. Again, the expert in most jurisdictions should be a physician with similar training and experience to that of the defendant physician.

2.8 – RES IPSA LOQUITOR

One exception to having a similarly trained physician testify (and in some states provide an affidavit prior to filing a formal suit) involves cases that fall under the category of **res ipsa loquitor**, which literally translated means "let the thing speak for itself." This is used when the alleged deviation from the standard of care is so egregious as to be blatantly obvious to the layperson (i.e. the judge and/or jury, called the **finder of fact** in these cases).

Although the four elements of a negligence case (Section 2.4) must be satisfied legally to have a *res ipsa loquitor* situation, there is shortcut. If, after you are told the story, you cringe, make a face, and mutter "Oh my Gosh!" then it is a blatant case. Examples include: amputating the wrong leg, operating on the wrong person, leaving various and sundry surgical tools in body cavities, etc.

Once a case is established as falling under *res ipsa loquitor*, the standard of proof shifts to the defense. Rather than the plaintiff having to prove negligence by the preponderance of evidence, the defense must prove that negligence wasn't a factor.

2.9 — Vicarious Liability

This term describes the additional liability that a person or organization (other than the defendant) may face in a negligence action. The reason that vicarious liabilities have taken on such an important role is principally what is known as the "deep pockets" theory of negligence lawsuits. Willie Sutton aptly stated this principle when he was asked why he robbed banks — *"Because that's where the money is!"* A good lawyer will aim charges of negligence at the deepest pocket available. This is done in the hope of obtaining the largest possible settlement. There is the additional psychological advantage of identifying the defendant as a faceless corporation rather than the individual physician. A jury may be hesitant to find an individual (particularly a physician) guilty if the case is "iffy," but is much more likely to find for the plaintiff if a wealthy corporation is the defendant.

Still another reason for an attorney to pursue the largest entity possible involves the potential for punitive damages. A jury would clearly request significantly higher punitive damages from a corporation worth hundreds of millions of dollars than an individual with a much lower net worth. This is a principle seen frequently in product liability cases.

In the deep pockets approach to civil litigation, the attorney for the plaintiff will always try to include the organization with the largest financial reserve. Federal and state governments, like other large organizations, are considered to have some of the deepest pockets around. An example of current deep pockets litigation involves tobacco companies. No lawsuits have been brought against individuals who may have had a role in "distorting the truth" in these cases. Punitive damages against large managed care corporations follow the same rule. Frequently the doctor, the hospital staff, the hospital that granted the doctor privileges, the parent organization, etc. will all be named in a lawsuit, with the expectation that some of the above may be dropped as the process proceeds. In a medical negligence suit, any healthcare provider holding privileges and whose name appears in the medical record is typically mentioned at the outset of the lawsuit. Only those that are found to meet all four of the required arms of a negligence case will actually be named in the final lawsuit. Two terms you may hear are **apparent** or **ostensible agency/authority**. These terms mean that a reasonable person would assume that an organization would in some way be responsible for the defendant's actions (even if they ultimately are not). For example, an organization offering ER services with contracted staff may be found to have vicarious liability if a person treated in that ER might reasonably believe that the staff member worked for the organization, rather than a contractor.

2.10 — Respondeat Superior

Similar to vicarious liability, **respondeat superior** refers to the principle where a "master" may be held liable for the acts of his "servants" (sound like your residency?). Employers can be held responsible for the negligence of their employees, and are frequently found to be. This means that doctors may be held liable for the acts of their employees or others under their supervision. Keep this principle in mind if **physician extenders** are employed in your practice. This is also an important consideration when psychiatrists are members of "treatment teams" but are unaware of the supervisory responsibilities for those practicing under their licenses.

This "captain of the ship" doctrine also applies to academic medicine. Staff physicians who work on wards where residents actively provide care, and in particular where medical students treat patients, are subject to *respondeat superior*. This applies even when the supervision of students is delegated to residents.

2.11 — National Practitioner Data Bank

The 1986 Health Care Quality Improvement Act established the **National Practitioner Data Bank** (**NPDB**). It is administered by the Bureau of Health Professions of the Department of Health and Human Services, and began receiving reports in 1990. The NPDB was instituted to prevent doctors with substandard skills from hopping between states. A physician's name is required to be reported to the NPDB when:

- There is *any* award given to the plaintiff as the result of a negligence action (even a settlement with no presumption of guilt, or a $1 finding for the plaintiff)
- Any case of an adverse privileging action
- An action is taken by a state board of medicine against a licensed physician
- An action is taken against a member by a professional medical association

From 1990 to 1996, there were 145,299 reports made to the NPDB:

- 118,211 (81%) were malpractice payments
- 20,707 (14%) were licensure actions
- 5,963 (4%) were privileging actions
- 268 were from professional societies
- 150 actions involved the Drug Enforcement Agency (DEA)

Registered nurses and allied health professionals can also be reported. A parallel data bank established as part of the **Health Insurance Portability and Accountability Act of 1996** (yes, the same **HIPAA** you have come to know and love!) is the **Healthcare Integrity and Protection Data Bank** (**HIPDB**) to combat fraud and abuse in health insurance and healthcare delivery. Names are submitted to this data bank of physicians/organizations convicted of a fraud violation.

2.12 — Clinical Practice Guidelines

For the purpose of this discussion, **clinical practice guidelines** (**CPGs**) are any written instruction regarding the appropriate evaluation and/or treatment for a particular disease, diagnosis, or symptom complex. CPGs are also known by a variety of other terms: **practice**

parameters, **treatment pathways**, **medical guidelines**, and **clinical policies**. CPGs can reduce the incidence of substandard treatment, preventable errors, and minimize the use of defensive medicine (which comes with its own risks and costs). Practitioners must be aware of the guidelines that their facility, practice, county, state, specialty association, etc. has established for their scope of practice. If these guidelines are taken in the spirit that they are intended, they can be very helpful. While many physicians resent being told how to practice medicine, guidelines do not impose strict requirements for adherence. Prudent clinicians clearly document their rationale for providing a form of treatment that significantly deviates from established guidelines. Clinical guidelines are helpful when it comes to providing evidence that the standard of care was met. Of course, the converse can also apply when a CPG was in place and it wasn't followed).

2.13 — Nuisance Lawsuits

Nuisance lawsuits are those that are filed when the plaintiff may accept a settlement deemed by the defendant's insurer to be a lower amount than the cost of taking the case to a jury trial (even when the case is defensible). The monetary value of "nominal" or "nuisance" is based on the size or worth of the organization being sued, and can be over $50,000. A settlement payment can be made on behalf of a physician even if no negligent care was provided. Because of this, the physician may not get his or her day in court. Insurance companies weigh the cost of proceeding to trial against the amount of the proposed settlement. Their decisions are based on finances, not principles.

☞ **Caveat**

Check your professional negligence policy to see if you have waived the right to take an action to court if the insurance company decides to settle.

2.14 — Intentional Torts

Remember that there are **intentional** and **unintentional torts**. Most doctors are unaware of their risk of being sued for an intentional tort. If at all possible, the plaintiff's lawyer can (and usually will) submit a lawsuit involving both types of torts. Plaintiffs are not limited to only one course of action. An **intentional tort** involves intended, volitional conduct (which can be an action or an omission) by a person, with an increased certainty that harm will occur, and which results in injury to another person or her property. The distinction between an *intentional tort* and *negligence* involves:

- The degree of likelihood that something bad will result from the action or omission
- The person's intent

Most negligence actions are not considered to be intentional torts. There are several reasons why someone might initiate a lawsuit for an intentional tort:

- Relative ease of proof: The 4 D's do not need to be proven — all that is required to show culpability for an intentional tort is that the action occurred and an injury resulted; there is no need for an expert witness in these cases (since there is no standard of care issue)
- There is a much greater likelihood of the plaintiff receiving punitive damages in an intentional tort because of the foreseeability of an injury occurring
- The statute of limitations may not be limited to 2 or 3 years (the norm in most jurisdictions) from the time the patient knew, or should have known, of the injury

Intentional torts (even ones likely to be successful) against physicians are infrequent because these actions are not often covered by a physician's malpractice insurance policy. Resulting settlements are likely to be lower than pursuing other types of lawsuits. Although some plaintiffs file complaints "just on principle," the usual goal of a civil suit is to receive as much compensation as possible. Furthermore, most attorneys do not take cases unless they feel confident they can win, or at least obtain a substantial settlement agreement. A list of common types of intentional torts appears below.

- Abandonment
- Assault
- Battery
- Breach of Contract
- Defamation
- False imprisonment
- Fraud
- Libel
- Invasion of privacy
- Slander
- Sexual assault/battery
- Intentional infliction of emotional distress

Assault and Battery are discussed in the informed consent section (Section 3.1). Remember that any non-consensual touching can be considered battery (e.g. performing surgery without proper informed consent). Assault is defined as the threat to cause harm.

Defamation/Libel/Slander/Invasions of Privacy are addressed in the confidentiality violations Sections 3.8 and 3.9.

Sexual Assault & Battery are presented in the boundary issues section (Section 3.14). An interesting legal strategy can develop when a physician is charged after having sex with a patient. Rather than charge the doctor with sexual battery, he may be charged with "mishandling the transference" (particularly if he is a psychiatrist). This becomes a matter of "medical negligence" instead of an intentional tort, and therefore is covered by malpractice insurance. How creative!

False imprisonment is covered in Section 3.7.

Intentional infliction of emotional distress is interesting, in that *anyone* can use this as a catchall category if they believe "they've been done wrong."

Breach of contract: A contract can be implied, verbal (as in a discussion with a patient), or written. Almost any doctor-patient relationship involves some form of implied contract. The patient agrees to come to you for an evaluation, provide their history, and comply with the agreed upon course of treatment. A physician agrees to provide quality medical care, answer questions, and not abandon the person. Some physicians make the mistake of promising a certain outcome, which occurs in a variety of forms:

- To a patient coming to you for treatment of major depression: *"If you take this medication you will feel much better in a short time."*
- To a patient with obesity: *"If you follow my regimen you will lose all the weight you want."*
- To a patient discussing a bone marrow biopsy: *"It will only hurt a little."*
- To a patient considering augmentation mammoplasty: *"You will be really satisfied and feel a lot more attractive."*
- To the family of an accident victim in the ER: *"We'll do everything possible to save her!"*

Within any specialty, there are many possible analogies to the above examples. The simplest guideline is to *never promise*. Even if you believe what you are promising, there are always some patients who don't read the textbooks!

Remember the "rule of thirds" in Section 1.4. For a breach of contract suit, all the patient needs to prove is that you promised something that wasn't delivered. A few jurisdictions require a written contract, but in most you can be sued for breach of a verbal contract. Examples of appropriate (and safe) responses in the above scenarios are:

- The depression patient: *"The majority of patients with symptoms like yours begin to get some relief over the course of several weeks."*
- The obese patient: *"If we work together on your nutritional and exercise regimen, I think you can achieve realistic results."*
- Pending bone marrow biopsy: *"The procedure can be painful, but we will provide several medications to reduce your discomfort and explain the process to you in detail."*
- Augmentation mammoplasty: *"We can review the probable physical results, but we need to discuss your desire for, and expectations of, the procedure."*

- The accident victim's family: *"I'm sorry — your family member is in critical condition. We'll do the best we can under the circumstances to save her."*

☞ **Caveat**

What you don't want to do is paint yourself into the proverbial corner and have to explain why a promised outcome didn't occur.

Several organizations have been successfully sued by patients and their families for breach of contract on the basis of not providing what was advertised in their pamphlets. Examples of problematic phrases are as follows:

- "All of our doctors are board certified"
- "Full range of wellness services available"
- "All mental health needs met"
- "Your doctor makes your treatment decisions, not an administrator"
- "*You* can choose your doctor"
- "Care available 24 hours per day"

2.15 — Regulatory Stuff

While the information that follows may at times seem outrageous, remember regulatory controls are one method of controlling healthcare costs while attempting to increase quality. Unfortunately, many innocent (or at least mildly oblivious) clinicians have been caught in the webs spun by regulatory agencies. Physicians are more likely to encounter liability difficulties from regulatory agencies than from any other source. The regulatory arena is ground that has become increasingly fertile and well-tilled in the past few years. The full harvest has yet to come. The contents covered are as follows:

- **Healthcare Fraud and Abuse Regulations:** False Claims Act, Medicare/Medicaid Fraud and Abuse Law
- **State Agencies:** Particularly boards of licensure, which oversee many issues that are considered to be professional negligence
- **Conflict of Interest Regulations:** Ethical Referrals and Anti-kickback Statutes
- **Other Regulations:** such as EMTALA, HIPAA, and ADA
- **Other Regulatory Agencies:** OSHA and EEOC
- **Regulatory Advisories:** Federal Register

2.15.1 – Federal Regulatory Agencies

There are many federal regulatory agencies involved in the practice of medicine. This may not surprise you. What may be surprising is that these agencies may have a far greater potential to seriously damage your practice and earning potential than a garden-variety medical malpractice suit.

2.15.2 – The Department of Health and Human Services

This is the principal agency involved in protecting the healthcare of all Americans, and providing essential human services. Some of the agencies which fall under the DHHS, are (in acronymical splendor): CDC, FDA, NIH, IHS, and CMS. DHHS had a budget for 2002 of $460 billion and employed 65,100 people. It is also the nation's largest health insurer — in 2002, Medicare processed 900 million claims.

2.15.3 – The Centers for Medicare & Medicaid Services

This body administers the Medicare, Medicaid, and Children's Health Insurance Programs and is one of the largest regulatory agencies. Until July 1, 2001, this organization was known as the **Health Care Financing and Administration (HCFA)**.

The **Office of the Inspector General** (**OIG**) investigates allegations of abuse. Felony violations are prosecuted by the **Department of Justice** (**DOJ**). Consider the following factoids:

* In 1999, the DOJ declared that healthcare fraud is its number two priority for the new millennium (right behind violent crime)
* The federal government committed $4.5 billion dollars between 2000 and 2006 to enforce various anti-fraud statutes

The anti-fraud statutes apply to anyone who receives funds from a federal agency (most notably from Medicare and Medicaid).

One of the most interesting of the federal anti-fraud laws is the **False Claims Act**. The original statute was passed during the Civil War to curtail the many suppliers who were charging the Union Army and federal government outrageous prices for supplies (this was the 1860's version of the $700 ashtray). The Act stated that it was illegal for anyone to knowingly charge the government more than an item was worth. The resurgence in popularity of this law occurred when it was updated in 1986 to have more teeth for enforcement. The federal government began to hold contractors responsible on many fronts for their overcharging practices. The term "whistleblower" entered our lexicon as someone who reported fraudulent activities to the government. Whistleblowers are officially known as **responders**. With the exponential increase in demand for medical care, the number of fraudulent claims being submitted under Medicare has also increased. The application of the False Claims Act to healthcare spending became a new and powerful focus. How does this apply to physicians? Few would argue that the small number of physicians who defraud the government *should* be held accountable for their actions. How does this pertain to the average physician?

☞ **Caveat**

There is no requirement on the government's part to prove that you *intentionally* committed fraud. Even if you unknowingly submit a false claim (and should have been aware of this), you can be fined. You can also be penalized for unfulfilled supervisory responsibilities. Further, the penalty can be a loss of your Medicare eligibility. Professional liability insurance will not cover your losses (or your legal costs).

2.15.4 – Formula For the Amount of the Fine in Fraud Cases

$5,000 to $10,000 per false claim

+

Three times the amount of the claim

If this isn't scary enough, there is another element. . .

2.15.5 – Along Comes HIPAA

Unless you have been living in outer Venusia for the past several years, HIPAA has become a major focus in all healthcare forums. This is also a program under the **Centers for Medicare and Medicaid Services (CMS)**. Healthcare fraud is estimated to amount to between $80 and $100 billion dollars per year, one-tenth of all healthcare spending!

The Kennedy-Kasselbaum Bill was passed in 1996 and is formally known as the **Health Insurance Portability and Accountability Act (HIPAA) of 1996**. HIPAA put new teeth into the False Claims Act by creating new healthcare fraud crimes, such as making false statements and embezzlement involving public or private healthcare plans or contracts.

The most recent focus of HIPAA is the requirement for compliance with the privacy regulations. *Every* physician and healthcare organization has been made aware of these confusing and seemingly overwhelming rules. HIPAA privacy regulations apply to all physician practices that use electronic medical records or electronic claims processing. The office needs to have someone train the staff on the privacy procedures and ensure compliance. The recommended steps include:

- Appoint a full-time or part-time person as the privacy official
- Develop the privacy policy for the practice
- Take reasonable steps to protect each patient's health information (limit access to patient records, ensure records are secure, etc.)
- Train employees about your privacy procedures
- Implement patient consent procedures for release of medical information
- Assess all business relationships where patient information is exchanged to ensure compliance

The compliance deadline for the privacy rules is April 14, 2003 for all covered entities except small health plans, which have one year longer. Further information on HIPAA compliance is available at many internet sites. Two recommended web sites are:

http://www.hhs.gov/ocr/hipaa/genoverview.html
http://www.hipaacomply.com

Most state medical associations also have helpful information about this topic. The only thing you should NOT do is assume you can ignore the rules. HIPAA has also extended the ability of many Americans to maintain their healthcare insurance after termination of employment, and to decrease the exclusions for pre-existing conditions. It is only upon reading the act in its entirety that the far-reaching consequences (tentacles?) become clear. The initial focus of the expanded fraud and abuse crackdown was aimed at laboratories. Settlements in these cases have reclaimed *hundreds of millions of dollars*.

2.15.6 – Qui Tam

A *qui tam* action occurs when an individual is granted authority (by statute) to bring a lawsuit against any individual or organization on behalf of the government. If the lawsuit is successful, individuals are given a percentage of the spoils. The infamous investigations of the 1980's in defense contracting were *qui tam* actions. Because of allegations of retribution against people bringing suit against their employers, the **Whistleblower Protection Acts** were passed. These acts prohibit retaliation after a complaint has been filed. *Qui tam* actions allow anyone to bring an action against you under the **False Claims Act**. A colleague, an employee, a patient, or anyone who has an axe to grind can launch a *qui tam* action. These actions are first reported to the DOJ, which investigates about 20% of all allegations. If the defendant is fined, the person bringing the action (the responder) gets 15 to 20% of the amount collected. If the DOJ does not pursue the action, the responder can bring a lawsuit to court. If the responder wins the civil suit, she can receive up to 30% of the award. *Qui tam* actions are increasing each year, as lawyers and others become aware of the possibilities. A search of *qui tam* on the Internet will return thousands of hits with hundreds of law firms. . . just waiting for someone to call. Consider the following knee-weakening scenario:

You have a part-time employee doing your billing. The CBCs and LFTs you have ordered over the past six months have been "unbundled" into their components (i.e. CBCs were billed as H/H, WBC, platelet count, MCV, MCH and MCHC; LFTs were billed as SGOT, SGPT, LDH and ALK PHOS). The difference between the CBC cost and the unbundled charges can be $50 (or more). For each unbundled claim, you can be fined up to $10,150. If this happened 20 times, you could be hit with a fine of $203,000 — for which you alone are responsible. In addition to fines (and occasional prison sentences), you may also lose your medical license, staff privileges, and your ability to participate in federal health care programs, particularly Medicare, Medicaid, and the **Civilian Health and Medical Program of the Uniformed Services** (**CHAMPUS**). This process is called being "*formally sanctioned and excluded.*"

☞ **Caveat**

The OIG of the DHHS has wide discretionary powers to exclude physicians for a number of offenses. In addition to being found guilty of violating one of the regulations or laws noted in this chapter, you can also be excluded for:
- Being convicted of a "controlled substances" offense
- Loss of professional license
- Submission of bills substantially in excess of usual charges
- Defaulting on student loans

The exclusion is usually for a fixed period (usually 5 years), and frequently results in disciplinary action by the state licensing boards, as well as a report being sent to the NPDB/HIPDB.

2.16 – Anti-Conflict of Interest Laws

Two laws regulating conflict of interest at the federal level are the **Anti-kickback Statute** and the **Ethics in Patients Referral Act**. Many states have similar statutes.

2.16.1 – Anti-kickback Statute

This is part of the anti-fraud and abuse provision in Medicare and Medicaid programs. This statute prohibits anyone from receiving monetary benefit (or any other type) from the act of referring patients when Medicare or Medicaid is paying for any service or item (or any part thereof). This is a felony punishable by up to five years imprisonment, or a fine of $25,000, or both.

2.16.2 – Ethics in Patient Referral Act

This act is also known as the **Stark Laws**, or **Stark I** and **II Laws**, named for Rep. "Pete" Stark. This act prohibits Medicare and Medicaid from paying for any service that physicians provide or order through an entity in which they have a financial interest. The goal of this act is to prohibit self-referral fees. **Stark I** was passed in 1989 and dealt primarily with laboratories. **Stark II**, passed in 1995, deals with everything else. In order to clarify what is allowable, the HCFA developed and published several exceptions (called **safe harbors**) to these laws. As of mid-2000 there were twenty-three. Dealing with these laws has become a legal subspecialty all its own, and another situation in which you don't want to rely solely on the advice of Cousin Joe. Given the massive confusion and murkiness over what is legal, HIPAA and the Balanced Budget Act of 1997 authorized individuals to request advisory opinions from the OIG, who will provide an opinion about whether an action will violate the Anti-kickback or Stark Laws. The catch is that those requesting assistance may well be investigated and prosecuted. You have the option of withdrawing your request before an opinion is formally issued. Also of assistance is the DHHS website: **http://www.dhhs.gov** — no fuss, no frills, no risk.

☞ **Caveat**

If you have to ask whether or not something is OK, it probably isn't.

2.17 — State Regulatory Agencies

Most states have their own variations of federal law, or have the authority to act on behalf of the federal government.

The one agency about which you will be most familiar is your state licensing board, usually called something like the Department of Professional Regulation. They can provide much of the state-specific information discussed in this book.

Most states also have their own prohibited referral and remuneration laws. These restrictions are available, along with all other regulatory information from your state board of medicine. A significant percentage of the published disciplinary actions against physicians are the result of violations of self-referral laws. Anyone can make a formal complaint about you to your state board of licensure. These complaints, often called **allegations of professional misconduct**, may result from:

- A specific case, such as an alleged act of medical negligence for which the plaintiff was unable to retain a lawyer
- A pattern of poor care
- A concern about an impaired physician or moral unfitness (usually a complaint related to a sexual relationship with a patient)
- Patient abandonment
- Performing unauthorized services

Once a complaint is filed with a state board, the allegations are usually heard before a committee. If the complaint seems unfounded or frivolous, it may be dropped. If, following investigation, the complaint is found to have validity, then the committee follows specific procedures for each stage of the investigation (and physicians are provided full due process). The penalties can involve:

- License revocation
- License suspension
- Reprimand
- Censure

Ensure that your legal counsel gets involved early in the administrative process (ideally at the time you are notified of a complaint). A claim of negligence to a Board of Medicine can also be used against you in a subsequent medical malpractice claim on the same issue.

☞ **Caveat**

Administrative actions can be more damaging (and expensive) than medical malpractice cases.

2.18 – EMTALA

EMTALA is the **Emergency Medical Treatment and Active Labor Act of 1986**. It is also known as the **Anti-Dumping Law**. It states that all hospitals receiving Medicare funding must provide medical screening for anyone who comes to the ER. EMTALA is enforced by the **Centers for Medicare and Medicaid Services** (**CMS**). Violations of EMTALA can result in civil actions brought forth by individuals or the CMS, who can impose fines up to $50,000 per violation (against the facility and/or the doctor), and can terminate the Medicare provider status of the hospital or physician. A civil action under EMTALA does not preclude a patient from filing a malpractice claim — in fact, most EMTALA lawsuits are coupled with medical negligence claims. EMTALA was enacted following several nasty cases when patients, who were unable to pay for medical assistance, were turned away from ERs without care. They either died or suffered serious injuries as a result of not receiving treatment.

Under EMTALA, after the required medical screening exam, if a patient is considered to have an emergency, certain steps must be taken. An **emergency medical condition** is defined as: *a medical condition manifesting itself by acute symptoms of sufficient severity including*

severe pain, psychiatric disturbances and/or symptoms of substance abuse such that the absence of immediate medical attention could reasonably be expected to result in: a) placing the health of the individual in serious jeopardy, b) serious impairment to bodily functions, or c) serious dysfunction to any bodily organ or part, or with respect to a pregnant woman who is having contractions (i) there is an inadequate time to effect a safe transfer to another hospital for delivery or (ii) that transfer may pose a threat to the health or safety of the woman or the unborn child."

Every patient who has an emergency medical condition must then be stabilized within the capacity of the institution, regardless of the ability to pay. The definition of **stabilization** from the statute is as follows: *Stabilization means, with respect to an emergency medical condition, that no material deterioration of the condition is likely, within reasonable medical probability, to result from or occur, during the transfer of the patient from a facility (or discharge).* This law also requires that specialists attend the patient as needed to assist with stabilization. To transfer a patient to another hospital the following conditions must be met:

- The patient must be stabilized (to the ability of the hospital)
- The patient must request and consent to the transfer
- If the patient is unable to consent, it must be in the best interests of the patient (the receiving hospital is better able to care for the condition), not because the hospital is inconvenienced by a non-paying patient
- The receiving physician must accept and agree to treat the patient
- The receiving hospital must agree to accept the patient and provide treatment
- The mode of transportation must be appropriate for the level of care necessary
- Copies of the medical record must accompany the patient

☞ **Caveat**

Any hospital or organization with an emergency room must be knowledgeable about the specifications of EMTALA.

A recent Supreme Court case ruled that the plaintiff does not need to show that there was an improper motive on the part of the defendant healthcare facility or physician, only that the care provided was different from that which would be given in a similar situation.

2.19 – Americans with Disabilities Act (ADA)

The 1990 **Americans with Disabilities Act (ADA)** guarantees certain rights for disabled individuals, and applies to organizations with 15 or more employees.

2.19.1 – Definition of the ADA

The ADA defines someone as "disabled" when he or she:

- has a physical or mental disorder that substantially limits one or more significant life activities,
- has a history of such a disorder, or
- can be perceived as having such a disorder.

There are four **titles** of the ADA: employment, public services and transportation, public accommodations, and telecommunications. The **Equal Employment Opportunity Commission** (**EEOC**) has the responsibility of enforcing the ADA. The ADA protects qualified individuals with disabilities who, with or without reasonable accommodation, can perform the essential functions of the employment position.

2.19.2 – Importance to Patients

The ADA plays a large role in protecting the rights of patients in many situations: insurance, ensuring actual physical access to healthcare facilities, protection from losing their livelihood based on a disability, eligibility for programs, etc.

2.19.3 – Importance to Physicians

In addition to providing protection for patients, the ADA protects physicians from negative decisions made by healthcare organizations, credentialing bodies, state medical boards, and other organizations if decisions are based on the presence of physical or mental disorders, and not simply impaired judgment.

Several cases that have gone to court because of wrongful denial of privileges/licensure were because physicians had psychiatric conditions, but with no evidence of impaired judgment.

2.19.4 – Bragdon v. Abbott

This 1998 Supreme Court case addressed the trend (being established by lower courts) that the ADA was providing less protection than intended. In 1994, a patient disclosed her HIV infection to her dentist during a visit to his private office in Bangor, Maine. She needed a cavity filled. Rather than performing this procedure at his office (as was customary), the dentist told her he would fill it only in a hospital setting, and that she would be responsible for the additional fees.

Ms. Abbott sued under Title III of the Act, which states that: *No individual shall be discriminated against on the basis of disability in the full and equal enjoyment of the goods, services, facilities, privileges, advantages, or accommodations of any place of public accommodation.* Public accommodation includes the professional office of a healthcare provider.

Before someone can receive protection under the law, she must meet the definition of disabled under the ADA. The Supreme Court had to decide whether an asymptomatic HIV infection was a *physical impairment* (point #1) that causes a *substantial limitation* (point #2) of one or more *major life activities* (point #3). The arguments in the lower courts were over whether an asymptomatic HIV infection substantially limits a major life activity. The Supreme Court, with three justices in dissent, found that HIV significantly limits sexual intercourse and reproduction. The court, not wishing their decision to be solely based on the limitation of reproduction, considered HIV seropositivity to have a profound impact on almost every phase of a person's life.

The result of this case is important to many HIV patients who wouldn't previously have been considered disabled if they were able to work, or their illness was controlled by medication. Every state has anti-discrimination laws. States may enact laws that are at least as protective of individual rights as is federal legislation. Some states also have HIV-specific statutes. The article by Gostin (1999) provides an excellent state-by-state chart. The state laws often provide protection for those individuals who work for organizations with less than 15 employees. Anyone in business (including healthcare) needs to have a clear understanding of the legal obligation to provide the services specified in the ADA.

☞ **Caveat**

If you are faced with a situation that you think might even be perceived as violating the ADA, check with knowledgeable legal authority. The philosophy that it is better to beg forgiveness than ask permission is NOT advisable in this case. . .

2.19.5 – Interpreters and Translators

Much can be learned from a 1998 lawsuit against a hospital initiated by a hearing-impaired patient who was not offered a translator skilled in **American Sign Language** (**ASL**). She was hospitalized against her will, but provided with neither medication nor treatment. She won the case.

A large number of organizations and offices are unaware of their legal obligation to provide communication aids and assisted listening devices. The web address **http://www.nad.org** provides information on this and other requirements.

2.20 – Occupational, Safety, and Health Administration (OSHA)

OSHA is an administrative agency under the Department of Labor. It regulates private sector workplace safety and health matters. Its goal is to maximize the safety of workplaces and minimize the injuries to workers. The bible for OSHA issues is the **Occupational Safety and Health Administration Compliance Assistance Authorization Act of 1998.**

OSHA's operating principle is that every employee has the right to a safe and healthful workplace. The majority of large healthcare facilities are aware of OSHA regulations, but smaller practices may not be. Even if you are in solo practice and have only one employee, the rules still apply. At the small practice level, common sense prevails: no holes in walkways, no wires strung across the room, no obvious safety issues. Physicians may encounter problems if, when a formal complaint is registered, numerous prior complaints were found to have been made on a local level and were not dealt with.

2.21 – Equal Employment Opportunity Commission (EEOC)

Many physicians are surprised at the number of complaints and lawsuits lodged annually under Title VII of the Civil Rights Act, which applies to all employers with 15 or more employees. The EEOC prohibits employment discrimination based on race, color, religion, sex, and national origin. Age is covered in a related act. Sexual harassment is also covered under this law. Since the mid-1990's, this area of civil litigation has become what one might term a "growth industry." What used to be termed "harmless sexual banter" is no longer overlooked or discounted. There have been several claims against physicians who continued to act inappropriately with female staff members. Adverse privileging and licensing actions have been undertaken for "unprofessional behavior." Furthermore, if a patient behaves inappropriately and offends a staff member, this can't be ignored either. If the patient does not stop the offending comments/behavior after being politely asked to do so, you are advised to take further action.

The hospital board/MCO can become the target of a lawsuit through **vicarious liability**. As in other employment cases, if the employer knew, or should have known of the offensive behavior, and did nothing about it, the case becomes difficult to defend. Physicians have taken organizations to court under Title VII for alleged discrimination and harassment. A good place to check for updates about regulatory matters is the **Federal Register**. Published weekly, this contains regulations from the DHHS. A periodic review will help ensure that you stay current with the items that are passed into law. For example, the Federal Register, on 7/2/99, published HCFA 42 CFR Part 482 — "Medicare and Medicaid Programs: Hospital Conditions of Participation: Patients Rights." This long publication promulgated guidance for the following requirements:

- Notification to the patient of his rights
- Exercise of his rights in regard to his care
- Privacy and safety
- Confidentiality
- Freedom from the use of seclusion or restraint in any form unless clinically necessary

Physicians who are unaware of these regulations are still held liable, resulting in potential lawsuits and possible exclusion from being able to participate in government programs.

2.22 — Professional Liability Insurance

Are you covered for the costs of legal defense in an administrative hearing before your state licensing board? What about your local privileging authority? Claims of fraud from a regulatory agency? Some policies provide limited coverage for these occurrences. For claims filed against you for violations of regulatory codes, you may be able to get something called a "billing errors and compliance" policy or clause. Even if you have made an honest mistake, you may still have to pay for your defense and be responsible for any penalties. Most insurance policies do not cover actions that involve dishonesty or fraud, just as medical malpractice insurance doesn't cover intentional torts. Discuss your coverage with an attorney knowledgeable in this area.

References

American Medical Association:
Beta-blocker Prophylaxis After MI.
Quality Care Alert. AMA, 1998

Americans with Disabilities Act.
42 U.S. Code, sections 12101–12111

Archer JD: **The FDA Does Not Approve Uses of Drugs**.
JAMA 252:1054–1055, 1984

Bragdon v. Abbott, 118 S Ct 2196 (1998)

Bryan v. United States, 118 S Ct 1939, 1946–1947 (1998)

Ethics in Patient Referral Act, 42, USC Statute 1395nn (1998)

False Claims Act, 31 USC Statute 3729 (1997)

Federal Anti-kickback Statute, 42 USC Statute 1320a-7b (1998)

Furrow BR, Johnson SH, Jost TS et al:
Health Law – Cases, Materials, and Problems, 2ⁿᵈ Edition.
West Publishing Company, St. Paul, 1991

Gostin LO, Feldblum C, Webber DW: **Disability Discrimination in America – HIV/AIDS and Other Health Conditions**.
JAMA 281(8): 745–52, 1999

Granville RL, Oshel RE: **The National Practitioner Data Bank Public Use File: A Valuable Resource for Quality Assurance Personnel and Risk Managers**.
Legal Med 98:4–9, 1998

Health Insurance Portability and Accountability Act of 1996.
Public Law, 104–191

Jacobsen PD: **Legal and Policy Considerations In Using Clinical Practice Guidelines**.
Am J Cardiol 80: 74H–79H, 1997

Kalb PE: **Health Care Fraud and Abuse**.
JAMA 282:1163–1168, 1999

Lipscomb J, Rosenstock L: **Healthcare Workers: Protecting Those Who Protect Our Health**.
Infection Control and Hospital Epidemiology 18(6), 1997

McCullough, Campbell and Lande: **Summary of Medical Malpractice Law**.
www.mcandl.com 1998, accessed 12/9/99

Public Law 105–241, 1998: Occupational Safety and Health Administration Compliance Assistance Authorization Act of 1998.

Scott RW: *Health Care Malpractice – A Primer on Legal Issues for Professionals*.
McGraw-Hill, N.Y., 1999

Simon RI: *Litigation Hot Spots in Clinical Practice*.
The Mental Health Practitioner and the Law.
Harvard University Press, Cambridge, 1998

Sage WM: **Fraud and Abuse Law**.
JAMA 282:1179–1181, 1999

Wing KR: *The Law and the Public's Health*.
Health Administration Press, Chicago, 1999

Woody RH: *Legally Safe Mental Health Practice – Psycholegal Questions And Answers*.
Psychosocial Press, Madison CT, 1997

3. The Doctor-Patient Relationship & Clinical Issues

The doctor-patient relationship and related issues overlap both medicolegal and ethical realms and are of prime importance to practicing clinicians. The topics in this section affect the multitude of interactions you have with your patients.

The scope of this chapter should not be considered to be all-inclusive, but presents the major areas in which clinicians need to have a good working knowledge. These areas include:

- **Informed Consent** (including determinations of the capacity to give informed consent)
- **The Right to Refuse Treatment**
- **Confidentiality** and **Privilege** (also addressed are typical exceptions for confidentiality and the duty one has to third parties)
- **End of Life Issues** (this section focuses on the most crucial issues, as well as those that are often misunderstood and ethically difficult)
- **Boundary Issues** (particularly sexual relationships with patients and dual relationships)
- **Abandonment**
- **False Imprisonment**
- **Good Samaritan Laws**

3.1 – Informed Consent

Probably the most important communication issue that occurs between physicians and patients involves **informed consent** (**IC**). While IC is well established as both an ethical and legal right of patients, its importance to successful doctor-patient relationships cannot be overemphasized. Autonomy and the right of self-determination of each person are the fundamental ethical principles that apply to medical practice. These principles are at the very heart of medical ethics, and can assist decision-making in difficult areas of practice. Justice Cardoza eloquently presented this concept in a 1914 case, *"Every adult person of sound mind has the right to establish what is done with his own body."*

The practice of sharing uncertainty with patients is crucial in medical decision-making. IC means a two-way communication, and is not merely a signature on a piece of paper. Clinicians who are comfortable with the IC process respect the autonomy of their patients. Respecting autonomy means that practitioners must *know and understand* what their patients want. This is different than *assuming* to know what they might want in a particular situation.

IC is a legal and ethical doctrine that requires healthcare professionals to educate patients about their diagnoses, and the risks and benefits of various treatment options. Once it is clear that patients understand these aspects, they are allowed to make their choices, and clinicians must respect these decisions.

3.1.1 – The Process of Obtaining Informed Consent

1. The patient is deemed to be capable of making medical decisions for himself (unless determined to be otherwise)
2. The patient is free of overt and covert coercion
3. The patient is fully informed about the following areas:
- the diagnosis and its implications
- the risks and benefits of the course of treatment being recommended
- the risks and benefits of alternative treatments
- the risks and benefits of receiving no treatment

The principle of **shared uncertainty** cannot be overemphasized. Almost everything that happens in medicine involves at least some degree of uncertainty. If patients understand the relative degree of uncertainty they face, they are much more likely to also accept the setbacks that may occur. Sharing uncertainty also distributes the responsibility between the patient and the physician on a more equal basis. In paternalistic times of yore, the doctor made the decisions and bore full responsibility for the consequences. This style of medical practice is no longer appropriate, nor is it wise.

3.1.2 — Development of Informed Consent

Until the 1960's most of the medical malpractice cases fell under the "Oh My Gosh!" category (e.g. amputating the wrong leg), known as *res ipsa loquitor* (discussed in Section 2.8). IC cases were the first medical negligence lawsuits not actually based on the *res ipsa loquitor* type of negligence. The standards currently in practice for IC cases developed primarily through several major precedent-setting cases. The presentation of three cases will illustrate how the current concept of IC developed, and highlight some of the ongoing problems facing clinicians.

Readers are reminded to check their state statutes regarding the exact requirements for obtaining IC. States vary significantly in their legal requirements, with most being at a lower level than the recommended ethical standards. When addressing IC issues with patients, a guiding principle is to consider what you would want the doctor to tell you, your spouse, parents, siblings, etc. about any particular diagnosis or choice of treatment.

The first major precedent-setting case was that of *Natanson v. Kline*, a 1960 action involving radiation therapy that went awry. Mrs. Natanson had a radical mastectomy in 1955 for breast cancer. She then received cobalt radiation therapy to the mastectomy site and surrounding areas. Subsequently, her skin, flesh, and the muscles beneath her arm sloughed. Some of her ribs became necrotic. She and her husband testified that while they were told that the cobalt treatment was new, they were not informed of any potential danger. Mrs. Natanson was also given an excessive amount of radiation. Amazingly, the jury found for the defendants (physicians) in this case. On appeal, the jury was given the instruction by the judge (not given in the initial trial) that: *"the doctor must advise the patient of the nature of the proposed treatment and any hazards of the proposed treatment which are known to the physician."*

This was the first specific court requirement for IC, and established what is known as the **reasonable medical practitioner standard**. This means that *physicians have a duty to explain to patients what a reasonable, similarly trained physician would tell them under similar circumstances.*

Another important result of this case was stated as follows (and echoes Justice Cardoza's comments): *"Each man is considered to be master of his own body and he may, if he be of sound mind, expressly prohibit the performance of even life-saving surgery. A doctor might well believe that an operation is necessary, but the law does not permit him to substitute his own judgment for that of the patient by any form of deception."*

This comment foreshadowed future legal rulings and is pertinent to the discussion of a patient's right to refuse treatment.

The **reasonable medical practitioner standard** was the accepted standard for informed consent until 1972, when the *Canterbury v. Spence* case established the **materiality of the information standard**. In this case, a 20-year-old male underwent a laminectomy for chronic pain. He was left a paraplegic. Afterwards, he said he was never told of the 1% risk of paraplegia accompanying the procedure. He also said that if he had been told, he would not have agreed to it. The *materiality of the information standard* means that *a patient must be told what any reasonable person would want to know to make a decision about the treatment or procedure.*

To have a successful case of medical negligence based on a violation of IC, it must be shown that the patient was not provided with the information mandated as necessary for that jurisdiction (a deviation from the standard of care), and that the inadequate or lacking IC was the direct cause of the damage. The *Canterbury v. Spence* case clearly illustrates this connection — the patient claimed that if he had been told of the 1% risk of paraplegia, he would not have had the procedure, and would therefore not have become paraplegic. While there are frequent oversights in the IC process, it must be shown that an injury occurred, and that the lack of informed consent was clearly connected to that injury.

Truman v. Thomas (1980) established the last aspect of the current requirements for IC. Dr. Thomas, a family practitioner, offered a Pap smear each year to Mrs. Truman. She declined the procedure because of the cost involved. She eventually developed an invasive cervical carcinoma and died. Her family sued Dr. Thomas, stating that he should have told her the risks of not having a Pap smear performed. He defended his actions by citing that the reason for having a Pap smear was common knowledge. The jury didn't agree. This case added to the IC requirements in that the risks and benefits (and prognosis) of *not* receiving treatment must be discussed, in addition to the risks and benefits of receiving a proposed course of treatment.

☞ Caveat

The responsibility for obtaining IC from the patient cannot be delegated, even to another physician.

3.1.3 – Ghost Surgery

Ghost surgery is a term describing an operation which is performed by a physician who is not named on the IC form. Remember, the assessment or treatment of patients without IC constitutes malpractice, and can actually make clinicians liable for the charge of battery, except where the law presumes consent (e.g. in an emergency). If the "right" surgeon operates on the wrong body part, or the "wrong" surgeon operates on the right body part, negligence can still be assessed in the event of an unfavorable outcome, though the other elements of negligence still need to be proven. Ghost surgery lawsuits can also be filed under breach of contract and won easily in court if a surgeon promised to perform the operation personally and didn't, or if the IC form doesn't include the surgeon who actually performed the procedure. The requirements for the type, scope, and documentation of IC vary widely between jurisdictions. The majority of states use the objective, or the **reasonable person standard**. These statutes are worded such that as long as a "reasonable person" would have consented to the procedure or treatment, then a legal action based on improperly obtained IC cannot proceed. This type of statute prevents many frivolous lawsuits based on IC issues, but does not ensure that physicians meet their ethical obligations. The majority of states require a signed IC form for all invasive surgical procedures. Signed forms are very helpful in defense arguments (even when doctors don't fully explain the diagnosis, procedure, risks, benefits, alternatives, etc.). Be cognizant of your jurisdictional requirements, but do not overlook ethical obligations. Remember that IC refers to the communication process you have with patients. It is best documented in conjunction with good progress notes, and is not just a signature on a form.

3.1.4 – Exceptions to Informed Consent

- Emergencies
- Therapeutic waiver
- Therapeutic privilege
- Implied consent

In emergency situations, the immediate care of the patient takes precedence over attending to procedural minutiae. If at all possible, try to obtain consent from the patient's family. Acts of *omission* are just as potentially risky as acts of *commission*. Furthermore, there is something particularly nasty about trying to defend a medical negligence case where the doctor failed to act because of what seemed like an administrative issue.

☞ **Caveat**

Remember that all patients deemed to be mentally competent can refuse even life-saving treatment.

Therapeutic privilege describes the situation where physicians believe that telling patients about their condition, or the options of treatment, will worsen the situation. This should be used very rarely (if ever), and limited to cases where it seems highly likely that providing information will be harmful to patients.

An example of therapeutic privilege involves a patient who is admitted to the ICU after a massive MI complicated by recurrent ventricular tachycardia. One might not want to mention that the MI has progressed until after the arrhythmia is controlled. An illegal and unethical use of therapeutic privilege would involve not telling a schizophrenic patient about the risk of tardive dyskinesia (which can occur following treatment with the traditional antipsychotics). A well-intentioned psychiatrist cannot use the exception of therapeutic privilege by saying, "if the patient knew about the risk, she wouldn't take the medication." It may well be that the patient wouldn't accept treatment even with the clear benefits that could be realized. Situations such as these are not considered a valid enough reason to take away a person's right to self-determination. If a schizophrenic patient lacks the capacity to make medical decisions, then her guardian/surrogate will make the decision (again, in accordance with the state laws that apply in this situation). You do not need to tell the patient about every possible side effect of a treatment or procedure, only the most common and the most serious ones. Remember to focus on the risks and benefits that a reasonable person would want to know to be able to make the decision.

Therapeutic waiver is the other exception to the legal requirement for informed consent. This occurs when a patient says that he doesn't want to be told anything about his condition or recommended treatment. If a patient says something like: "Oh doctor, I don't understand all of your medical talk and don't want to know. You're so smart – you make all the decisions for me." Look out! This situation is a potential landmine. If a patient says this, tell him that you believe it is much better for him to at least try to understand the treatment options, and to consider inviting a family member to join the discussion.

If the patient refuses to be involved in the process, and is competent to make that decision, get a witness (someone other than a family member) to corroborate your discussion. Make sure you document the conversation and the name of the witness in the medical record.

☞ Caveat

The type of patient who wants others to make decisions for her frequently possesses dependent personality traits, and may well harbor passive resentments as well. In the event of an unfavorable outcome, the patient and his or her family may become very angry. What you want to avoid is having this resentment directed at you, and eventually unburdened in the courtroom (i.e. "The doctor never told me").

The IC process is the cornerstone of good patient care, and this involves respecting autonomy. If the patient is part of the ongoing decision-making process, he very likely has a strong alliance with the treatment team, feels listened to, and is much less likely to pursue litigation as a course of action even in the event of an unfavorable outcome. When patients believe that they have been ignored, misled, given only cursory attention, or treated with disrespect, then angry (and litigious) feelings are likely to arise.

Implied consent. When a patient holds out her arm to get blood drawn, this implies consent for the venipuncture. Implied consent as an exception to IC covers undisclosed risks that are considered common knowledge (once again, by the omnipresent "reasonable" person).

3.1.5 – Documenting Informed Consent

Documentation plays an important role in IC and its many offshoots (such as the right to refuse treatment). More information on documentation is presented in Section 5.4.

Clinicians know that good documentation is imperative — not only as a risk management issue, but to ensure good patient care. Other providers need to know information about medications, allergies, diagnoses, etc. Unfortunately, many physicians have been exposed to the "castor oil" theory of documentation (i.e. if the documentation wasn't perfect, the entire scope of care was criticized). This approach is a demotivator for physicians (and may cause a "purging" of the desire to improve). When something unpleasant is forced on anyone, it is human nature to reject it, even if it might ultimately be something positive. The bottom line is:

- Good notes do help the patient
- If you didn't document it — "it" never happened
- Write smarter, not more
- If it can't be read, it won't help you or anyone else

As students, many physicians are told they needed better documentation skills. The natural reaction is to write longer notes. The phrase "just the facts, ma'am" is particularly valid here. You do not have to write a short story about the 15 minute talk you had with a patient, just the basics of their symptoms, your assessment, and management plan. If there was anything added to the treatment plan, a brief documentation of the IC process is in order. Most items need only a few sentences. It is particularly valuable to make a record of the questions that patients have. This provides clear documentation of the patient's participation in the IC process, and that you addressed his questions.

3.1.6 – An Example of Documenting Informed Consent

ID: 32-year-old married Chinese female followed for treatment of major depression. Takes only oral contraceptive pills. Denies any allergies to medications.

Subjective: Seen 2 weeks ago for symptoms of depression in the context of marital discord. Returns today after starting marital counseling. Currently suffering from insomnia (early a.m. awakening), fatigue, tearfulness, feelings of worthlessness, and diminished concentration. Denied suicidal ideation. No new stressors.

Objective: Neatly groomed, cooperative, appears tired; soft-spoken with psychomotor retardation (slumped in chair/slowed gait); "pretty down" mood with blunted, dysphoric affect — appropriate to expressed thought process. Denies suicidal ideation. No evidence of psychosis. Beck Depression Inventory Score = 28; TSH 1.2.

Assessment: Major Depressive Disorder, single episode, moderate severity, without psychotic features (DSM-IV-TR 296.22)

Management Plan:
1. Begin fluoxetine 20 mg, p.o., qam. Discussed most common side effects — sleepiness/anxiety, nausea/anorexia, headache. Explained other first-line meds and probable course with and without meds. Told she needed to stay on meds for 6 to 9 months after resolution of symptoms to decrease the risk of relapse.
2. Patient to call in one week; follow-up in 2 weeks. To continue marital/individual counseling.
3. Patient to call in the interim with any questions/concerns.
4. Agreed to contact me, call 911, or go the ER if she develops suicidal ideation in the interim. She is capable of making treatment decisions.
5. Patient Education: Watched videotape on depression – expressed surprise at how classic her symptoms were and said she felt more hopeful after seeing her tape.
6. Patient expressed an understanding of the above treatment plan and process of recovery.

3.2 – Competence/Capacity to Make Medical Decisions

While the exact wording of IC statutes vary between jurisdictions, there is one absolute. For IC to be considered valid, the person giving it must be competent to do so. All adults are presumed to be competent unless there is a legitimate reason to think otherwise. This is a protection provided by the ethical and legal doctrine of **self-determination**. Because of this, most physicians don't mention that the patient had adequate decision-making capacity when IC was obtained. However, making a notation in the medical record that a patient was deemed capable of providing IC can be very beneficial.

Cases where competency is a potential issue usually involve the following situations:
- A patient agrees to a treatment that has a low potential benefit and a moderate potential risk
- A patient refuses a treatment that has a low risk and a significant potential benefit
- The patient's family disagrees with the treatment plan
- The patient agrees to a research protocol

- The patient's record has evidence that could raise the question of competency (e.g. a nurse's note recording decreased cognitive awareness at night, after meds, etc.)
- IC was given after the patient took medication that could affect memory, judgment, cognition, etc. (to avoid this situation, it is best to have the IC discussion before the patient receives medication)
- Any other situation where you want to make sure the patient is competent to provide informed consent

Additional information about competency determinations is as follows:
Competence refers to having the capacity to understand and act reasonably. Competence is a legal term, and the decision about someone's competence is made by a judge.
Capacity is having the mental ability to make a rational decision (based on understanding and appreciating all relevant information). Capacity is determined by a clinician.

There are many different types of competency (over 30) that can be adjudged. In general, when there is more at stake for an individual (e.g. loss of life or liberty, finances, etc.), a higher level of evidence indicating competence is required.

Each of these competencies is assessed by balancing an individual's constitutional rights against local laws and the interests of society. In most jurisdictions, attending physicians are legally able to be the capacity assessors for their patients. However, the majority of physicians, unless trained in the assessment process, do not understand how to proceed, and are wise to request assistance from a consultant. When a consultant (usually a psychiatrist or psychologist) is asked to do a "capacity assessment," it is important to clarify which type of capacity needs to be assessed, and for what specific reason. These are crucial elements, because capacity is specific to a person's decision-making ability for a *specific task* at a *specific point in time*. (e.g. to assess Mr. Langerhans capacity to consent to an ERCP scheduled for tomorrow). There are many mental health professionals who do not know how to conduct capacity assessments. For this reason, it is prudent to ensure that your consult request is directed to someone who has the proper training and experience.

An error frequently made by clinicians is to equate a patient's decision-making capacity with her performance on the **mini-mental state exam** (**MMSE**). While most researchers agree that scores of less than 20 out of 30 on the MMSE provide a fairly good correlation with a lack of decision-making capacity, this alone is not sufficient. Up to one-third of patients with impairments in their decision-making ability (overlooked by physicians) will score between 20 and 30 on the MMSE. Many people have impaired decision-making abilities that are disguised by the cognitive abilities that remain intact.

The capacity to make medical decisions balances the competing interests of doing no harm to the patient against preserving the right to self-determination. The principle at the heart of informed consent is that each person, while deemed competent, has the right to make decisions regarding her medical care, even if others consider these decisions to be unwise. This is at times difficult for physicians to accept.

Many authors who write in the area of medical decision-making capacity believe in the usefulness of a "sliding scale" where different types of capacity require varying levels of decision-making ability. In other words, the more there is at risk for the patient, the more physicians will want to be certain that the patient has intact decision-making capacity. While a sliding scale is not an officially recognized legal consideration, it does have widespread acceptance.

3.2.1 – Example of a Sliding Scale for Decision-Making Capacity

A patient is offered a medication that will likely cause few side effects, and is potentially of life-saving benefit. Here, a physician might be less concerned about the patient's capacity to accept treatment because there is little risk involved and considerable benefit. However, when a treatment is proposed that has high likelihood of causing side-effects or complications, coupled with little potential benefit, it is critical to establish that the patient is competent to make medical decisions.

A major undertaking in the study of capacity determinations has involved the participation in clinical research. This is a particular concern when the research subjects have questionable capacity (e.g. involuntary patients or those with mental impairment) or where there is the potential for coercion, or even the *perception* of coercion. Doctors who recruit their own patients for research that they themselves are conducting must be careful. Should patients feel even the slightest degree of coercion, physicians may be on shaky ethical and legal grounds. Patients may harbor covert fears that by not participating they may fall out of favor with their doctor, and compromise the quality of their care. Many physicians consider it a conflict of interest to recruit their own patients.

Capacity assessments have been performed for decades on two groups of patients — those participating in clinical research and those who have been hospitalized on an involuntary basis, usually on psychiatric units. However, in other areas of medicine, this has been a relatively recent focus. For readers interested in this area, the reference section lists articles by Drs. Appelbaum and Grisso that are of particular assistance. While several approaches for conducting capacity assessments exist, the schema provided by these authors has been widely used and validated, and is easily integrated with the legal standards for competency.

3.2.2 – Elements of a Capacity Assessment

Since competence is a legal term, most jurisdictions require that patients demonstrate the following capabilities in order to be considered competent to make medical decisions:
- The ability to express a choice (Section A)
- The ability to understand the information (Section B)

- The individual's ability to appreciate the information as it applies to her specific case (Section C) — this is not required in all jurisdictions
- The ability to reason with the information (Section D)

A. The ability to express a choice involves the patient *being capable* of making a decision about his care, *arriving* at such a decision, and *informing* someone of that decision. This is not always as simple as saying yes or no. Patients do not necessarily have to communicate their decisions verbally. Patients on ventilators may be able to communicate via blinking, writing, hand squeezing, etc. Non-verbal patients are frequently written off as being unable to participate in healthcare decisions. A more subtle problem arises with submissive, dependent individuals who are unable or unwilling to make decisions. In situations involving ambivalent patients, the underlying cause of their uncertainty needs to be explored. Is it because the individual received new information and made a valid reassessment of the situation? Or is it because auditory hallucinations are confusing him? Again, the sliding scale of competency is an important consideration.

If someone is completely unable to express a choice because of a mental or physical illness, then a guardian needs to be appointed to make medical decisions. If a patient is merely ambivalent, or has trouble making decisions, the resolution depends on the degree of risk involved in the decision. A referral to a psychiatric colleague can be particularly useful in cases where the etiology of someone's ambivalence is unclear.

B. A patient's ability to understand information is the aspect of capacity that receives the most attention from physicians. If it is obvious that the patient doesn't understand what the physician is saying, the issue of IC is called immediately into question. At some point during the interview, a physician will ask, "Mr. Jones, do you understand the things I've just told you?" If the patient says "no," or has a blank stare, few doctors would be comfortable with a signed consent form. Ask patients to repeat back to you what they have heard you explain.

C. The next item is often less well understood or considered in the process of capacity determination. In addition to understanding the information provided by physicians, a patient must be able to

appreciate how this information pertains to his case. While a patient may seem to be cognitively intact and have a good understanding of facts presented, he may not appreciate how the facts pertain to him specifically. An example is as follows: Mrs. Brown is in the ER for evaluation of a possible placenta praevia. She seems to understand the need for an emergency cesarean section. The difficulty arises when her doctor leans forward to get her signature after detailing the risks to her, and she states, "Wait a minute! I understood what you were saying doc, but it doesn't apply to me — I'm not pregnant!"

Frequently, people with delusional disorders, selective neurologic deficits, etc. appear entirely normal. Their lack of decision-making capacity goes unrecognized unless a thorough assessment is undertaken.

D. The final aspect of assessing capacity is an evaluation of the patient's **ability to reason with the information provided**. This is particularly important when a patient makes a choice that is not seen as reasonable, or not one that most people would make. As long as a patient can coherently explain why a certain choice is being made, provide a clear understanding of the possible implications, and demonstrate how the situation applies to her personally, then physicians must respect the choice being made.

Competence to make medical decisions is an increasingly important concept for physicians to understand, practice, and document. It is crucial for anyone performing a capacity assessment to ensure that the patient has been fully informed about her condition and proposed treatment beforehand. Sitting in with the treating physician and listening to the information provided is one way of accomplishing this. If you are the treating physician who has requested the consult, it can be very helpful to go through the elements of informed consent with the patient one more time. It is perfectly appropriate to re-educate someone again at the time of a capacity assessment.

The goal of the informed consent is to support the autonomy of patients, and as far as possible, allow them to make their own choices. You don't want to remove their right to make decisions unless there is clear evidence of incapacity.

3.3 – Research

Much has been written in the area of the ethical, legal, and moral rights and wrongs of performing research on those who may be only marginally competent (or even incompetent). Even for clearly competent patients, many checks and balances are available.

There is a particular department under the **Department of Health and Human Services** (**DHHS**) that oversees research conducted with federal funding. This is the **Office for Protection for Research Risks** (**OPRR**). Many federally funded organizations have received suspensions for a variety of violations, such as the use of ineligible patients, coercion, or using inadequate means to obtain informed consent.

Most organizations are required by policy or law to have strict processes in place to oversee human research. This may include a Committee for the Protection of Human Subjects, an **Institutional Review Board** (**IRB**), etc. All human research funded by the DHHS and the FDA must be approved by an IRB.

The University of Rochester has a unique training program. The principal researchers must take an exam (and score at least 85%) to have their studies made eligible for IRB review. The OPRR is available to answer questions about specific situations, from either IRB members or individuals.

Recent protocols on Alzheimer's disease (AD) patients are illustrative examples of competing ethical issues and their appropriate resolution. On one hand, patient rights activists are vocal about protecting individuals who lack the ability to give informed consent. On the other hand, patients in the early stages of AD (and a different set of activists) state that not performing research on this disabling illness is discriminatory.

Like all other issues where the rights of individuals are considered, the potential benefits must be weighed against foreseeable risks. The **National Institute of Mental Health** (**NIMH**) has developed a protocol that satisfies both groups. Patients in the early stages of AD are assessed for their capacity to consent to participate in research studies. While still able to make decisions about their treatment and research involvement, they appoint a surrogate to make these decisions for them when they are no longer able to do so. There are many safeguards built into this process, such as not performing a procedure if there is evidence that the subject is in any kind of discomfort, etc. The NIMH has developed a very satisfactory approach by using **advance directives**. These allow patients to maintain their autonomy and protect those who do not have adequate decision-making capacity.

Patients must be free of coercion in order to give consent to participate in research. Previously, a large amount of research was conducted on captive populations — prisons, mental institutions, and the military. The past few decades have seen huge legal changes designed to protect the rights of these populations. The Nuremberg Principles, developed after the atrocities performed in the name of research during the Holocaust, are used by many organizations to ensure adherence to the highest ethical standards.

Even if DHHS funding is not provided, it is appropriate to follow their basic guidelines and use JCAHO standards for guidance, whether or not you are part of a JCAHO-accredited organization.

Concern about coercion also applies to individual physicians who conduct research, particularly regarding recruitment. How can physicians recruit subjects from their own patient pool without even the slightest degree of coercion? Even if a physician says, "I made sure she knew she didn't have to participate," many patients have a desire to please their physicians and are afraid that their care might suffer if they don't participate. Research efforts have also focused on patients with psychiatric illnesses and their capacity to give consent to participate in research studies.

3.4 – Minors

Physicians who care for minors and adolescents need to be aware of both state laws and local facility policies regarding the capacity to consent to research, obtaining informed consent, etc. In most jurisdictions, the parents are the child's guardians, and have decision-making responsibility. If the parents are divorced, the parent with primary custody has the responsibility for consenting to treatment. Be aware that you cannot release information to the non-custodial parent without proper consent.

While parents ultimately make decisions for minors, physicians should still make every effort to explain the diagnosis and treatment to the child. Even though the legal decision-making responsibility lies with the parent, there are ethical responsibilities to both to the parents and to the child.

Economic informed consent refers to the ethical requirement to disclose all appropriate treatments, not only those authorized by the patient's health plan. Physicians should also disclose any potential financial gain they will receive from recommending treatment options. This is an ethical, and in some cases, legal requirement.

☞ **Caveat**

A valuable question to ask patients is what their expectations are for treatment. For example, ask the following questions, "What does success mean to you in this situation?" or "What do you hope to get from treatment?" This will help differentiate what you think success is from what the patient envisions.

An example is as follows. A 68-year-old cancer patient has a reasonable chance of surviving for several years by accepting an aggressive chemo/radiation therapy regimen that will make him feel lousy. When you ask this patient what he hopes to gain from the treatment, he may state, "I want to have a few good pain-free months to spend with my family and finish a few paintings." This informs you which aspects to emphasize in your discussion about treatment options. You can still offer your preferred treatment plan, but you now know where the priority of the patient lies — quality vs. quantity of time remaining.

Another suggestion is to ask patients to list their top three priorities or goals in seeking medical care. For one it may be minimizing pain, another to allow mobilization, and others would want to be able to live independently.

3.5 – The Right to Refuse Treatment

The right to refuse treatment is intertwined with the informed consent process, but at times seems much less straightforward. Remember, the autonomy of the patient reigns supreme in making medical decisions when the patient is deemed competent. It is every person's right to make unwise decisions and to refuse treatment that may even be lifesaving. In the latter instance, the patient is choosing one of the treatment alternatives, which is to receive no treatment. Right to refuse treatment issues are on a continuum with right to die issues, which are addressed in Section 3.10.

3.6 – Leaving Hospital Against Medical Advice

Some patients want to leave the hospital when it is **against medical advice** (**AMA**). An example of this situation is as follows:

It is Friday night at 8 p.m., and you are trying to finish your rounds and leave. You are called to see a patient (not your own, of course) who is having a heated discussion with a nurse. The patient ripped out her IV, and has her angry spouse with her. The nurse hands you an AMA release and asks you to have Mrs. Jones sign it. This situation is a set-up for an unfavorable outcome, which may well be accompanied by lingering feelings of animosity. It doesn't have to be this way. One approach to this problem is as follows:

First, get a concise history about what is going on. Then, see the patient immediately, and say something like the following: "Hello Mrs. Jones, my name is Dr. Wear-Finkle (shake hands). I hear that you wish to leave the hospital. Is it OK if I talk with you for a few minutes?" At this point sit down across from Mrs. Jones and ask "Can you tell me what is upsetting you and why you want to leave the hospital?"

Your job in this encounter is to attempt to understand why Mrs. Jones wants to leave. It often has nothing to do with quality of care issues, but rather a negative personal interaction with one of the staff, possibly coupled with anxiety. You can take the interaction from an adversarial one to at least neutral ground. If the problem cannot be fixed with an empathetic and non-challenging intervention, and you believe that Mrs. Jones is competent to make an informed decision to leave the hospital, then she can of course leave. It is important that you ensure that she knows the following (which you document in the record):

• Her diagnosis
• The reasons you recommended further hospitalization
• The risks she faces by leaving without continued treatment
• She is welcome to return to the facility for further treatment
• The symptoms for which she should seek immediate care and the risks of ignoring these symptoms
• Other possible places she can receive treatment if she chooses not to return to your hospital

Any resemblance to the previous procedure of documenting IC is entirely intentional! The AMA process is the same as informed consent. A competent patient has the right to choose between the available treatment options — with one of these options being to decline treatment altogether.

If your organization insists that the patient sign an "AMA Form" then ask her to do so. Simply state that the form is a record that the patient understands she is leaving against the advice of medical personnel. Much more important than this form is a well-written note in the medical record containing the points listed above. Note the patient's capacity to make this decision, particularly if she is refusing treatment that places her at high risk upon leaving the facility. Physicians cannot prevent a competent patient from leaving the hospital, even if this decision appears to be an act of poor judgment. If the patient's competence is in question, perform a capacity assessment, and follow your organizational and jurisdictional guidelines.

3.7 – False Imprisonment

False imprisonment occurs when a competent patient is prevented from leaving a healthcare facility, or is committed to an institution in violation of state law. Patients do not have to be locked in solitary confinement to be falsely imprisoned. If physical restraints are applied or someone is forcibly prevented from leaving the ER and there is no legal reason for this, the person can sue everyone involved for both false imprisonment and battery. False imprisonment actions make for clear and simple, no-fuss lawsuits. This is an intentional tort, not a negligence action. There is no requirement to prove the *dereliction of duty/direct causation of damages* aspect — only that the person was restrained against her will without justification.

A tragic case that clearly illustrates this issue is one of a 29-year-old woman with a life-long history of asthma. She presented to an ER for treatment and authorized only treatment with oxygen, but was given both oxygen and another medication by nebulizer. She developed a headache from the medication, removed the mask, and expressed her desire to leave the ER. The staff was concerned about her oxygenation status, and the doctor felt she would need to be intubated. He told her he would treat her in a conservative fashion. The patient and her sister didn't trust the doctor and decided to leave. They were stopped at the exit by a security guard and the doctor, and forcibly separated. The patient was physically restrained and intubated. She did not give consent for the intubation. When she was released from the hospital the next day, she felt traumatized, and stated she would never again go to a hospital. Two years later, she again had a severe attack and refused to go for treatment. When she lost consciousness, an ambulance was summoned, but she died two days later.

Her father sued the physician and the hospital for the events that had transpired during the initial ER visit. His lawsuit alleged wrongful death, negligence, assault and battery, false imprisonment, and a violation of his late daughter's civil rights. The trial judge instructed the jury that a patient has the right to refuse medical treatment except in a life-threatening emergency situation. The jury found for the defendants. On appeal to the Supreme Judicial Court of Massachusetts, the lower court ruling was reversed. To this court, it was clear that a competent patient has the right to refuse treatment, even when faced with a life-threatening situation.

3.8 – Confidentiality

"Three may keep a secret when two of them are dead."
Benjamin Franklin

COnfidentiality is the **C**linician's **O**bligation to keep information obtained in a professional relationship from third parties, unless the patient authorizes its release. This is both an ethical and a legal requirement. Breach of confidentiality suits are not unusual. Even if the physician was not directly involved, he or she may be considered responsible because of the principle of vicarious liability (remember the deep pocket theory of litigation from Section 2.9). For example, if the event in question was due to a negligent office practice or an action by one of the staff, the physician can still be held liable. The deeper pockets of the healthcare organization, if it didn't ensure that its policies were clearly promulgated, could also be targeted in a lawsuit.

Some of the most common places where breaches of confidentiality occur are the hospital cafeteria, elevators, and doctors' offices. A rule of thumb is to assume that the person standing next to you in a public place knows the person whose case you intend to discuss and will repeat exactly what you said. Don't leave medical records in sight of anyone who may be in your office (and may get nosy if you leave). Politely ask someone to leave your office if you need to take a call.

One surprising tidbit to consider if you are responsible for the confidentiality of an office practice is the following: if your administrative staff did everything correctly with regard to not leaving records out, but forgot to lock the area where the records are kept, you may still be liable. If someone enters a closed area and opens an unlocked file cabinet to view a record that is in your safekeeping, *you are liable*, not the trespasser. Even though the other person was trespassing, as long as he didn't have to "break and enter" to gain access to records, the responsibility is yours.

3.8.1 – Information Management

This is a huge new area in both medicine and office management. Electronic records present valuable opportunities to improve care, but also many possibilities for breaching confidentiality. If you are making the transition to an electronic record in your practice, ensure the software company has clear procedures to safeguard the security of the information. See Section 2.15.5 regarding HIPAA.

3.8.2 – Frequently Overlooked Areas

Telephone answering machines

What is your arrangement for voice mail? Is the answering machine in a secure area? If not, is the volume turned down? Who listens to the messages and where does this occur? The important thing is to ensure that only those who have a need to know information about patients are in a position to hear it.

Computer security

Who has access to the computers? Are patient records (and other sensitive information) protected by a password?

Computer servicing

What happens when the computer needs to leave the office to be serviced? What about the personal records on the hard drive?

Medical records in filing cabinets

Although it is hard to imagine someone rifling through records, it does happen. Back-up computer disks should also be kept in a locked area.

Day-to-day practice

When patients enter the office, are there patient records open (or even on your desk if you leave the room)? Is any patient information on the computer screen?

Voice pagers

Make certain that the volume is turned down so the incoming message is not within earshot of others. If the lab announces your CEO's positive gonorrhea culture over your pager during an executive meeting, this can be a career-limiting event.

Disposal of confidential information
Ensure the process that you think is happening is actually taking place. It is not unheard of that medical record contents are sorted into piles by prisoners and sold to the highest-bidding recycler.

3.9 – Exceptions to the Confidentiality of Medical Information

The legal requirement for confidentiality does not apply in the following situations:

Duties to Third Parties
• When your patient is a threat to others

Mandatory Reporting
• Communicable diseases
• Child or elder abuse
• Impaired driving
• Any other mandatory reportable item in your jurisdiction

Mandatory reporting can be a very sticky area — know which statutes say "shall" or "may" or "shall not." If you fail to report something when you are required to do so, you may face disciplinary action. Alternatively, if you make a report and are not required to, or are prohibited from doing so, you may face civil action. In Florida, for example, spouse abuse cannot be reported without the victim's permission. The requirement to report gunshot wounds or other wounds indicating violence is in force only when the physician was actually called to treat the wound, not finding it as an incidental discovery during an exam for another problem.

3.9.1 – Court-Ordered Requests

These can occur as part of any criminal trial, a civil suit, or at the request of an administrative body (like a licensing board or as part of a workman's compensation hearing). The crucial issues in this instance are that you:
• Inform the patient about the limits of your confidentiality
• Outline exactly who will have access to the written report
• Discuss the potential impact of the evaluation

Clearly, informed consent is required to be able to conduct the evaluation. Several physicians have been burned by doing an evaluation for a worker's compensation claim, releasing the information to the employer, and then being sued for breach of confidentiality.

3.9.2 – Patient-Litigant

This means that the patient has raised the condition(s) for which you are treating them as part of litigation. Once the individual has placed his or her condition *at issue*, you are no longer bound to keep information confidential (in reality, it means that privilege can no longer be invoked — this is described in Section 3.9.9). Despite this, seek legal counsel before releasing any confidential information.

3.9.3 – Dual Agency

There are several settings where the physician has a duty to both the patient and an organization. This most frequently occurs in prisons, the military, and schools. The patient should be told ahead of time by the doctor that the usual level of confidentiality does not apply in this particular situation. Again, this is principally an issue of informed consent. Most physicians working in these environments are aware of their ethical duties to the patient populations they serve. It may come as a surprise to many who do not work in these systems, but there is a strong focus on the preservation of individual rights in spite of the competing interests.

3.9.4 – Duties to Third Parties

This term refers both to the duty to protect others from the actions of your patients, and the legal duty you may unintentionally incur from your actions. It is important to have an awareness of both factors, and to be able to distinguish between the two. Psychiatrists and other mental health professionals are well aware of the duty they have to third parties when one of their patients indicates the desire to harm another person. This **duty to warn/duty to protect** a clearly identifiable third party from harm is addressed in all state legislation. This duty developed from the 1974 and 1976 Tarasoff cases.

Individual state requirements vary widely. Even in states where the statute is worded to say that an identified victim "may" be warned "if" the patient has the means and "is more likely than not to act on the intent." Common sense dictates that at some point there is an ethical duty to protect others. This surpasses the patient's right to confidentiality — statute or no statute. Know your state laws and then decide what you can live with.

☞ Caveat

"I would much prefer to defend a breach of confidentiality suit than a wrongful death suit!"
A Famous Defense Lawyer

Courts have usually used common sense (yes, it's true) in the above situations. They will usually side with the clinician who acted in good faith to try to protect others.

☞ Caveat

All duties to third parties are based on protecting identifiable or, at times, even non-identifiable persons from the foreseeable harmful acts of your patients.

As noted above, a duty can be established when you have knowledge that your patient poses a foreseeable risk to others (either identifiable persons, or the general public). The extent and scope of your duty in different situations is dictated by state and case law. A good example is the risk of HIV+ patients transmitting the virus. Some states require reporting or notification of the sexual partner. Some states allow physicians to make the notification, while others forbid notification altogether.

3.9.5 — Release of Information to Third Parties

Whatever your practice milieu, it is prudent to know your facility guidelines regarding release of information to third parties. Always ask patients to sign a release of information form. As with all forms that may have eventual liability importance, legal counsel should check it for completeness and appropriateness.

☞ **Caveat**

Except in rare situations, do not release any patient information without a signed consent.

There are limited situations where a physician can release information when not authorized to do so by the patient:

• *State Reporting Requirements*. All states have a variety of required reports. These include, but are not limited to: communicable diseases; child, spouse or elder abuse; gunshot wounds; etc.

• *HIV*. Know your local reporting requirements. Violating established HIV reporting procedures is a major potential liability issue.

• *Department of Motor Vehicles (DMV)*. Many states have mandatory reporting for several conditions, while others require that the department be notified of those for whom there is a concern, and then they conduct an investigation into the person's ability to safely operate a vehicle.

Notifying the DMV is not always a clear-cut decision, and involves weighing the evidence for impairment against removing a personal freedom. The best way for any physician to deal with these issues is to discuss matters with the patient. In many instances, the patient will be reasonable and agree to give up driving or restrict her time on the road. The second avenue of pursuit is to include family members. If there is still concern, tell the patient that you are notifying the DMV. If you have dealt with this matter in a fair and progressive manner with the patient, you are unlikely to be faulted for erring on the side of safety.

3.9.6 – Minors

Familiarize yourself with your state laws regarding the release of information involving minors. Be clear as to whether your patient may be an **emancipated minor**, a finding that is adjudged by a court. Emancipated minors have all the rights of adults (other than age-restricted activities). They absolutely have the right to not have any information released to their parents without their written consent.

If you have a moral dilemma by not including the parents in the evaluation or treatment of a minor for sexually transmitted diseases, substance abuse, contraception, etc., encourage the teen to agree to include one parent. If this is refused, you can either treat the person or make a referral to someone who is comfortable with the situation. As long as this is not an emergency and you've made sure that someone else is available to the patient, you have satisfied your duty.

3.9.7 – Other Third Party Liability

In your relationship with a patient, a duty may be established to a third party if advice is given to this person/agency, or if the third party is somehow included in the treatment plan. Whether or not your actions established a duty (making you liable for a possible negligence action) is determined by a court. Examples of this liability are as follows:

A. In 1980, a woman was told by her internist that she had syphilis (from a lab result). The physician told her to tell her husband so he could be treated. Both spouses blamed each other for being unfaithful, which led to a divorce. Two years later the lab informed the physician that there was an error. The doctor called the patient, and both she and her ex-husband were understandably peeved. The husband then brought suit against the doctor, the lab company, etc. In this case, duty was established because the physician advised the patient to tell the husband. It is easy to extrapolate from this case to some of the potential minefields present in everyday practice.

B. In 1993, a man from Tennessee died from a non-contagious disease (Rocky Mountain Spotted Fever). His wife subsequently died as well, and an action was brought against the doctor. The court stated the physician had a duty to warn the wife that she was at risk because the ticks that transmit the disease "tend to cluster." There are not a lot of "clustering ticks" sort of cases, but beware. It does make one speculate about how absurd things can become.

All four negligence elements — **duty**, **breach** (dereliction), **direct** (proximate) **cause**, and **damage** — must be satisfied. The controversial element in third party liability suits is that of duty. In the cases where there is the risk of violence, many state statutes establish the presence of duty. In the two cases discussed above, there are no pertinent statutes that would have clearly established a duty to a third party.

3.9.8 – Duties to Non-Identifiable Third Parties

These duties vary by state, but generally you can address your duty to non-identifiable third parties by warning the patient. These considerations include any illness or medication that may affect a patient's ability to drive safely, discovery of a genetic disorder that could affect other family members, use of medications under hazardous conditions, etc.

For example, consider a situation where you prescribe a medication that may be sedating. You would advise the patient that it may make him drowsy, and therefore he shouldn't drive after taking it. You then document that you explained the possible hazards to the patient. If he uses poor judgment and drives, and causes an accident where someone is injured, the patient is the culpable party. You are not liable for prescribing a sedating medication. The only catch occurs if the patient is not mentally competent to understand your instructions.

3.9.9 – Privilege

Unlike **CO**nfidentiality (which is the **C**linician's **O**bligation), **PR**ivilege belongs to the patient (the **P**atient's **R**ight). If a patient exerts her privilege, this prevents the physician from disclosing any information obtained during the course of evaluation and treatment. Privilege usually becomes an issue during litigation or in other legal settings. This is not something that physicians are involved with during day-to-day practice. It is incorrect to say that you can't divulge information about a patient because it is privileged (again, privilege belongs to the patient). If the patient was not available to make a decision regarding the release of information, and it was your belief that releasing information would be harmful, you can consider invoking privilege on the patient's behalf (through your lawyer).

3.9.10 – Subpoenas

Most physicians at some point in their practice will receive a subpoena related to a patient's litigation (hopefully not against you). A subpoena may be served in person or can be sent as a regular letter. The subpoena will state exactly what is required, which is usually that you, the physician, release a medical record to the court or appear in court.

☞ Caveat

It is advisable to have a lawyer that you can contact with day-to-day questions in addition to the one your insurance company assigns if you are named in a malpractice suit. Your personal lawyer should be knowledgeable in all aspects of medical negligence and in the other legal problems a physician can face (intentional torts, administrative hearings, etc.). This individual's primary responsibility is to you, not to the healthcare organization or the insurance company.

Many physicians are confused about their duty regarding the confidentiality of medical records after being served with a subpoena. Must one respond and provide everything requested in a subpoena? Yes, and no. You have a legal duty to respond to the subpoena, but you don't necessarily have to do what the subpoena states, nor should you in many cases. A subpoena is issued when a judge agrees that the information requested by an attorney could reasonably be considered pertinent in a lawsuit. A subpoena is different (and on a lower level) than a court order. Here is one way to proceed upon receiving a subpoena:

1. Notify your attorney and your insurance company.

2. Contact the patient and request that he or she sign a release of information form authorizing the release of the information requested. When patients take legal action against someone, it is often their attorneys who request the information, so it is not usually a problem to obtain consent for the release of information.

3. If the patient refuses to authorize the release of information or doesn't answer your request, you can then respond to the subpoena by stating that the patient may want to exercise his or her privilege, and the court needs to decide if it wishes to override this. You must respond to a subpoena. After you submit your request to the court, the judge will then either cancel the subpoena or direct you to provide the information through a court order.

4. If you receive a court order, you *must* respond. Failing to release information can bring a charge of contempt of court, leading to a possible fine or imprisonment.

A variation in this process that you may encounter is a *subpoena duces tecum*, which is a subpoena to report in person at a certain time and place, and to bring specific information with you, which is usually a medical record. When you appear with the record (or other information requested), you do not need to actually turn over the information unless ordered to by the court. The mistake some physicians make is that they hand over the record to the first person who requests it without checking to see if this person actually has the authority to receive the information. Unfortunately, there are some lawyers who take advantage of inexperienced physicians. Again, it is imperative that you obtain legal counsel as soon as you receive a subpoena.

3.10 — End of Life Issues

An area that has received an increasing amount of attention has been the rights of individuals (and their families) when death is near. Some important end of life issues are:

- The Right to Die
- Physician-Assisted Suicide
- Hospice
- Ethics Committees
- Advanced Directives/Durable Powers of Attorney

End of life issues are an area of medicine with many ethical and legal considerations. Ethicists involved in this area may overestimate the level of understanding that an average physician has regarding these issues. It is crucial to be aware of which aspects fall on the ethical "slippery slope." Many doctors have conservative views on end of life issues, often based on the fear of litigation.

3.10.1 — The Right to Die

Much has been written about one of the most basic issues involving self-determination, the right to die. Supreme Court decisions have (almost) sanctioned this as a constitutional right because this concept can be considered an extension of the right to refuse treatment, which is constitutionally protected. The major focus in end of life issues is generally on the right of competent individuals to refuse even life-sustaining treatment. The decisions of legal cases and legislation in all states support the autonomy of competent individuals to direct their medical care.

3.10.2 – Is There a Difference Between Withholding and Withdrawing Life-Sustaining Treatment?

This issue is frequently brought to ethics committees, and is generally an issue such as, "Mrs. Smith was supposed to be a 'no-code,' but she ended up on the respirator and now we can't take her off. What should we do now?" These cases are similar to the right to refuse treatment situations, although many physicians have trouble looking at it from this perspective. The dilemma appears to involve situations where a patient expresses a desire to halt life-sustaining treatment already in progress. Many clinicians believe there is a difference between stopping treatment that has begun, and not starting treatment in the first place. This is not so. In situations involving competent individuals, or incompetent individuals who have clearly communicated their wishes through living wills (or have surrogate decision makers for healthcare decisions), the process is straight-forward.

☞ **Caveat**

There is no difference, ethically or legally, between not starting and stopping a life-prolonging treatment. It can be helpful to look at this concept in reverse. If there was a difference, and in some way it was more legally or ethically risky to stop a life-prolonging treatment, rather than not start one, physicians might be less likely to initiate treatment.

Pragmatically and legally, there is no difference between acts and omissions that have the same outcome. As the court said in the *In Conroy* case: *"Whether necessary treatment is withheld at the outset or withdrawn later on, the consequence — the patient's death — is the same."*

A typical treatment algorithm recommended by ethicists (and lawyers) for **do not resuscitate** (**DNR**) orders reads as follows:
If the patient with a terminal condition does not desire to be intubated and everyone agrees it would not reverse the condition, then everyone is usually comfortable not initiating treatment. But, if there is a disagreement between either the family and patient or physician, then the patient can be intubated while the situation and decision is re-evaluated. If there was the fear that "once intubated, always intubated," the decisions would become harder.

For elderly patients who have conditions that will likely result in death within a short period of time, there is usually support for the wishes of patients who have advance directives stating the patient's wishes for life-saving measures. The concept of "futility" is widely discussed in the literature, but is not an operationally useful term because it lacks a precise definition. Many physicians and staff who provide care to patients with terminal conditions use futility to mean that treatment is unlikely to restore health or an quality of life, and that it will accomplish little more than allowing the person a brief extension of life. An ethically difficult case might involve a patient with end-stage cancer who refuses to make an advance directive, and who arrives in the emergency room already having been intubated by the EMTs. In this situation, the patient's family and physician can usually provide guidance on how to proceed. Another difficult situation is sometimes termed "The Daughter From California." This scenario has both the person's family and the treatment team in agreement that life support should be stopped. However, the long-estranged daughter arrives (and as Murphy's Law would have it, is usually either a physician or a lawyer), refuses to give permission and threatens to sue the hospital if mom or dad is taken off of life support. The best way to handle any difficult case is to involve a member of the institution's ethics committee.

3.10.3 — More Tough Cases
- A Jehovah's Witness patient who will die without a transfusion
- A quadriplegic patient on a respirator who wants it turned off
- A teenager in a chronic vegetative state whose family wants to cease enteral feedings

These are some of the cases that go to the courts, where the following factors are considered:

The individual's rights and autonomy
vs.
The state's interests:
- Do no harm
- Preserving life
- Ensuring the ethical bases in clinical practice are followed
- The duty to prevent suicide
- Innocent third parties should be protected

The courts generally tend to support the right of a competent patient to refuse or stop treatment, even if it is life sustaining. This is applied particularly if the patient has a terminal illness, has a diminished quality of life with minimal hope of improvement, or if the treatment itself can be difficult to endure. Two of the most important right to refuse treatment/right to die cases are those of *In re. Quinlan* (1976) and *Cruzan v. Director* (1990). Both cases revolved around the wishes of the family to discontinue life-sustaining treatment for their daughters. The major issue centered around trying to determine what the patient would have chosen if she had been competent to make the decision. The *Cruzan* court found that each person's decision to refuse consent to any invasive act — including the delivery of food and water — was constitutionally protected. However, in this case, the court supported the state's right to require evidence as to the wishes of the incompetent person (at the standard of **clear and convincing evidence**). Most courts do not lump hydration and artificial nutrition in with comfort care, they consider it a life-sustaining medical treatment, which can be refused like any other treatment.

3.10.4 – Advance Directives

An **advance directive** allows a person to extend decision-making autonomy from the present to a time when he or she may be deemed incapable. All 50 states have statutes authorizing some form of advance directive. Forty-six states allow both a living will and durable power of attorney for healthcare. Part of the **1990 Patient Self Determination Act** was to require healthcare institutions to provide written information to patients at the time of admission regarding their right to refuse treatment, and their right to establish an advance directive. Every state makes available to patients a form for executing an advance directive. These forms are in all hospitals, and several books have been published to guide patients through this process.

☞ Caveat

An advance directive that is legal in one state may not be in another. Attempts are being made to ensure that all states will recognize the person's expressed wishes, but if you have a patient from another state, you may want to advise them to check on whether their advance directive will be respected elsewhere.

3.11 – Physician-Assisted Suicide

Proponents of **physician-assisted suicide** advocate this act for patients with terminal illnesses who are in severe, chronic pain. The AMA and several other organizations have decreed that assisted suicide is not compatible with the healing role of physicians. What these organizations do advocate is careful attention to the needs of the patient — addressing both better pain management and palliative care.

3.11.1 – What Is Physician-Assisted Suicide?

Physician-assisted suicide (PAS) involves physicians *assisting* in the dying process. This needs to be distinguished morally, ethically, and legally from **euthanasia**, which is directly causing another person's death. The increase in activism by both patients and physicians led to the **Oregon Death With Dignity Act of 1996**.

Patients and their physicians have challenged state laws prohibiting physician-assisted suicide. Most notable are the two cases reviewed by the U.S. Supreme Court in 1997. These cases did not lead to a ruling on the issue of PAS, but rather found that a person does not have a constitutionally protected right to kill himself.

- *Washington v. Glucksberg* involved a lawsuit initiated by several patients and their doctors who challenged state bans that violated their due process liberty interest under the 14th Amendment.
- In *Vacco v. Quill*, there was a challenge to the New York law prohibiting PAS. The claim was that the law violated the 14th amendment equal protection clause for those desiring PAS.

The Supreme Court found that neither case involved a violation of any constitutional right. This finding did not, per se, prohibit any state from passing a law allowing PAS, but stated that challenges on the above grounds were not valid. What the Supreme Court clearly took a stand on was that physicians have a duty to aggressively manage a terminally ill patient's pain: *"It is widely recognized that the provision of pain medication is ethically and professionally acceptable, even when the treatment may hasten the patients' death, if the medication is intended to alleviate pain and severe discomfort, not to cause death."*

And from Justice O'Connor: *"A patient who is suffering from a terminal illness and who is experiencing great pain has no legal barriers to obtaining medication from qualified physicians, even to the point of causing unconsciousness and hastening death."*

What has been an undisputed positive outcome of the Right to Die/PAS debate is the advancement of education and knowledge about pain management, and the treatment of depression in terminally ill patients. Ongoing dialogue has been enhanced in many forums.

There have also been several papers published with guidelines on how to handle requests for PAS and treat the terminally ill. Singer (1999) identified the following points for enhancing the quality of care at the end of life:
• Receiving adequate pain and symptom management
• Avoiding inappropriate prolongation of dying
• Achieving a sense of control
• Relieving burdens
• Strengthening relationships with loved ones

End of life duties to patients are increasingly recognized as ethical obligations.

3.12 – Ethics Committees

Every organization should have a mechanism by which ethical concerns can be addressed. A hospital will have a formal **Institutional Ethics Committee** (**IEC**) with a membership that usually includes the following: physicians (primary care, intensivist, psychiatrist), risk manager, nurse, lawyer, chaplain, administrator, social worker, and other members the group deems appropriate. More important than the titles or positions are personal characteristics: ethical assessment skills, process skills, and interpersonal skills.

This is not the type of committee that members should be under duress to join — participation should be voluntary. The IEC members will be adept at dealing with the various ethical issues that arise in an organization, and which commonly involve end–of–life matters. Even organizations without a formal committee (usually smaller ambulatory care practices) should have a process in place to address the issues that do arise. **The American Society for Bioethics and Humanities** (or a similar organization) can provide guidance.

3.13 — Hospice

Hospice programs offer the terminally ill the best opportunity to exercise their autonomy and maintain their dignity at the end of life. Hospice care is interdisciplinary, provides support for the entire family, and is much better positioned to provide the appropriate care for the dying through palliation of their symptoms.

Few would argue that a person enrolled in a hospice program has a better exposure to medical professionals who are knowledgeable about pain management, palliative care, and are comfortable with the legal and ethical issues surrounding end-of-life decisions. Unfortunately, only a small number of individuals who could benefit from a hospice program take this opportunity.

A large part of this problem can be explained by the difficulty in making accurate medical prognoses. For patients to be eligible to receive hospice care under the Medicare Hospice Benefit, their physicians must certify that the person is terminally ill, and has a life expectancy of six months or less. Up to 50% of those who are terminally ill in the U.S. are not offered the opportunity for hospice enrollment. The majority of those entering hospices have made the decision so late that they may only have weeks left to live.

Some physicians are unaware of the range of services hospices offer. Others are averse to telling patients about their terminal status (due to a concern over the patient's fragility, or possibly their own discomfort). Physicians may think of hospice care only for cancer or AIDS patients, when there are patients with many terminal conditions who could benefit greatly from these programs. Some physicians are also reluctant to prescribe the palliative care recommended by hospice medical staff because it focuses on symptom improvement only, not treating the underlying disease.

Physicians trained in palliative care focus on alleviating suffering instead of the prolongation of life without quality. Pain management is performed effectively. Parenteral fluids or enteral nutrition is rarely recommended. These interventions are made only when an identified symptom can clearly be improved. Some physicians are uncomfortable unless they can provide all possible treatments for patients (even those who are agreeable to do-not-resuscitate (DNR) orders).

Hospice care will ensure that patients and their families understand the levels of available care. Staff will prepare family members for the day when the patient develops respiratory distress. This preparation includes documents, MedicAlert® tags, etc. to have handy so that if an emergency response team is called, they will be informed about the patient's living will and DNR request.

If you are ethically committed to preserving a patient's dignity throughout his lifespan, an awareness of, and involvement with, hospice programs is essential. Failure to discuss palliative care options, and particularly failure to properly manage pain, may result in a legal action against you, though these issues are perhaps more ethical in nature. Recently, a state board of medicine took formal action against a physician who under-treated several patients in need of aggressive pain management.

3.14 – Boundary Issues

Boundary issues can be divided into two varieties, **boundary crossings** and **boundary violations**. These terms originate from mental health parlance and describe a spectrum of behaviors ranging from marginally inappropriate behavior to the clearly inappropriate relationships that occur between doctors and patients. This spectrum runs from mildly ill-advised actions to those that can result in felony convictions.

3.14.1 – Boundary Crossings

Boundary "crossings" are minimal transgressions of the ethical guidelines that address the doctor-patient relationship. Such boundaries are established to ensure that there is not even the perception that a physician has breached the strict fiduciary responsibilities of trust and confidence, and never puts personal interests ahead of those of the patient.

Boundary issues are most strongly emphasized in mental healthcare, but are certainly applicable to all physicians. The more conservative physicians are, the less likely they are to find themselves in legal difficulty. Some of the healthiest risk management attitudes and behaviors you can have toward your patients include:

- Do not develop personal relationships with your patients
- Avoid doing the following with patients: going out for meals, having a drink, entering into business relationships, having them to your house, giving or accepting gifts (other than those with limited value). Now, of course common sense must apply — if you live in a small town and the majority of the citizens are your patients, it is unrealistic to expect that you will not establish some type of relationship with them.
- Never share personal information with a patient, this intimates a friendship instead of a professional relationship
- Don't touch patients except to perform a physical examination. Again, use common sense. A hand on a shoulder for encouragement, or holding a dying patient's hand is not what this recommendation advises against. While *you* might see a hug as being entirely non-sexual and merely supportive, the patient may not.
- Don't make exceptions in your schedule for select patients
- Don't agree to see only certain patients after hours — this is frequently a prelude to a boundary violation.
- Don't set different fees for different patients. This practice is not advised unless it is based on a patient's ability to pay, and is then applied to everyone in a particular income category. Waiving the

co-pay or giving professional courtesy may actually be a violation of state or federal regulations.
- Maintain a stance of neutrality
- Provide quality care, demonstrate empathy with your patients, and offer support for the decisions they make as competent and autonomous individuals. Don't give advice or tell them what they "should" do (other than the obvious things like stop smoking, get more exercise, buckle up, etc.). Do not recommend they get a divorce, quit their job, or sue their mother!

At times boundary crossings are acceptable, some examples are:
- Giving an elderly patient a ride home on an icy day
- Sending a card expressing condolences over a family member's death
- Sending a gift, or attending the wedding of a patient's only child

In these situations, a physician is clearly putting the best interests or safety of patients first.

3.14.2 – Boundary Violations

The majority of boundary violations begin quite innocently. Drs. Simon and Gutheil note that for mental health professionals, most boundary violations begin "between the chair and the door," when the physician lets her guard down with idle chit-chat. The most serious of all boundary violations, and the one having the greatest impact upon the practitioner and patient, is having sexual relationships with patients.

☞ Caveat

Never have a sexual relationship with a patient. This is the number one boundary violation that can cause you to lose the farm — or at least your medical license. The prohibition of physician's sexual contact with patients dates back to the Hippocratic Oath: *"I will come for the benefit of the sick, remaining free of all intentional injustice, of all mischief, and in particular of sexual relationships with both female and male persons, be they free or slaves."*

For psychiatrists and other mental health professionals, having a sexual relationship with a current patient represents the gravest error in judgment possible. A psychiatrist having sex with a patient is committing a felony in at least twenty states (at the time of writing). This number is expanding. Minnesota has a mandatory reporting law (if a patient tells her current psychiatrist that she had sex with her previous psychiatrist, the second psychiatrist is required to report it).

Legal restrictions on doctor-patient relationships exist because one member (the patient) cannot make a free and competent choice. These laws stem from the same prohibition of sexual relations between adults and minors. Many of the state laws have wording taken from prohibition of incest statutes.

It is also unethical and/or illegal for a mental health professional to have sex with a former patient (again, state statutes vary on this point). Many states have what is called a "perpetuity" rule, meaning that *once someone is a patient, she is always considered to be a patient.* The perpetuity rule has widespread support. It is difficult to justify, in a specified period of time, that the power imbalance in a therapeutic relationship will change because physicians are put in special positions of trust.

There are also practical issues involved. Ask any lawyer if a problem exists in becoming romantically involved with former patients, and a wise response will be *"Not if you live happily ever after."* If you marry a former patient and don't live happily ever after, your soon-to-be ex-spouse may well claim that you took advantage of her vulnerable position as a patient. In addition to the divorce settlement, you may be sued for a variety of things and be reported to your state board of medicine.

A not infrequent dynamic is one where a patient interested in pursuing a relationship with her physician may go through an initial period of idealization. All goes well until the physician does something the patient doesn't like, such as trying to end the relationship. This brings about a very potent devaluation that can lead to many personal and professional problems.

One self-report survey of physicians who admitted to having sex with one or more patients during their careers revealed the following:
- All primary care physicians   10%
- Obstetrician-gynecologists   18%
- Psychiatrists   5%

This information, and the fact that having sex with a patient currently under your care is grounds for action to remove your license, is reason to take heed. Most specialty societies are currently discussing this issue in their ethics divisions. While there is no debate on the ethical transgression of having sex with current patients, there is considerable discussion about establishing guidelines regarding former patients. In a successful 1998 lawsuit against a healthcare professional for having sex with a patient, the court held that: *"If a medical professional not practicing in the field of mental health enters into a relationship of trust and confidence with a patient, and offers counseling on personal matters to that patient, this is taking on a role similar to that of a psychiatrist or psychologist, and that professional should be bound by the* same *standards as would bind a psychiatrist or psychologist in a similar situation."*

Using this reasoning, it is easy to see where a lawyer will attempt to hold all physicians to the standard to which psychiatrists are held (that sexual relationships are illegal, not just unethical). Family physicians prescribe more antidepressants in the U.S. than do psychiatrists. As is appropriate in many cases, the primary care provider treats patients for depression or anxiety disorders.

Once a psychiatric diagnosis is made and treatment is provided (e.g. "supportive psychotherapy"), primary care providers may well be held to the psychiatric standard if they have sexual relationships with patients.

☞ **Caveat**

Several profiles have been compiled of physicians at risk for sexual misconduct. Some of these features are: male, ages 40 – 50 years, marital discord, and alcohol abuse/dependence. The majority of physicians who were charged with sexual impropriety (and lost their licenses or received prison sentences) did not believe they were at risk for having sexual relationships with patients.

Usually there is a progression of boundary crossing along a slippery slope of unethical behavior. At some point the acceptable doctor-patient boundary is breached, and this eventually progresses to a sexual relationship. This process can begin by calling a patient by her first name, or accepting a gift. . . then running into her after work and sharing a drink. . . then offering her a ride home, agreeing to see her in the evening when the staff have gone home. . .

Limit your relationship with any patient to one of professional intent only. You want to avoid any speculation about your ability to be completely objective in your role as a physician.

3.15 — Standby

A **standby** is a person who is present during a medical exam. Any organization accredited by JCAHO must have policies in place regarding standbys. The patient has the right to request a standby of the same sex, and the physician has the right to refuse to do a physical exam if a standby is not present. It is prudent to have a standby present when examining a patient's breasts or genitals. The presence of a standby should be offered even when the physician and patient are of the same sex. Standby personnel should be present at any time you feel uncomfortable with a patient — from outright flirtatiousness to situations where you just have a gut feeling that something isn't right. The patient has the opportunity to request a standby. Your policy should be prominently displayed in your office, and can be part of the posted patient rights and responsibilities. Do not use a patient's spouse or friend as the standby, even if it is more convenient than using one of your staff. If a standby was present for an examination, add her name to the medical record.

3.16 – Dual Relationships with Patients

This section covers any relationship a doctor has outside of a typical doctor-patient relationship. The guiding principle here is the same as for sexual relationships with patients. . . *don't get involved in these situations.* Examples of ill-advised dual relationships, even for non-psychiatric physicians, are:

3.16.1 – Developing Close Friendships With Patients

There are many pitfalls in befriending patients, a key being confidentiality issues (particularly if mandatory reporting is involved). Any relationship presents a potential conflict of interest, especially when patients expect special treatment. However, this recommendation doesn't mean that you must decline every social invitation if you live in a small town and many community members are your patients.

3.16.1 – Involvement in Business Ventures With Patients

If there is an unfavorable outcome from a business venture, the patient can sue you because she felt coerced and that her medical care might have suffered if she didn't agree with your suggestions. In many instances, physicians get into trouble because they are trying to be helpful. Provide your help and support as a physician by practicing the highest quality of medical care possible, not as a friend or business partner.

3.17 – Abandonment

Many clinicians believe that once they have established a relationship with a patient, it cannot be put asunder. Physicians who believe this will be pleasantly surprised that our system truly does support the rights of all parties — doctors included. Once you have established a duty to a patient, you do have one absolute responsibility, which is to provide that patient with the standard of care for his evaluation and treatment. You are not compelled to continue this relationship when it is not in the best interest of either party. There are a variety of situations when it is perfectly appropriate for you to consider terminating a doctor-patient relationship. There is only one absolute — *after establishing a duty to a patient, you must provide care in emergency situations and offer alternative treatment options for that patient.*

Physicians are liable for charges of abandonment if they do not meet the criteria listed below. Remember that intentional torts are not usually covered by malpractice insurance coverage. Some of the more appropriate reasons to terminate your relationship with a patient are:
- The course of treatment is completed (the most common reason)
- You are retiring or moving
- The patient exhibits continued non-compliance with medical treatment
- The patient has engaged in repeated harassment of you or your staff
- The patient engages in persistent seductive behavior
- The patient is not being honest about medical matters

In each case, the patient must be provided with written notification that you are withdrawing from her care. If at all possible, discuss this on the last scheduled visit or send a letter.

☞ Caveat
In every case, send a letter via certified mail with a return receipt requested. The letter should state (at the minimum):
- That you are no longer going to continue providing medical care
- The reasons why care is being withdrawn; this is not necessary in all cases, but is recommended if the reasons are not likely to be inflammatory
- State that you will provide any needed care for a short period of time while he finds another physician (usually 30 days)
- List alternatives for care, and include names and phone numbers
- Outline what the patient should do in case of an emergency

3.18 – Good Samaritan Laws

Every state has some form of Good Samaritan Statute that applies to those who respond to the scene of an emergency. The details vary, but all provide some form of immunity from claims of negligence for those who render aid in an emergency without a specific duty to do so. These statutes are in place to encourage physicians (and others) to assist in an emergency without incurring legal risks. While physicians are encouraged to assist in emergencies, there is no legal requirement to do so. Once a physician stops at the scene, she needs to remain there until help arrives (of an equal or greater ability to assist).

Closing the gap in the liability coverage of physicians responding to an emergency occurred when the **Aviation Medical Assistance Act of 1998** was passed. As part of this law, there is Good Samaritan liability language that protects any healthcare provider who is "licensed, certified, or otherwise qualified to provide medical care in a state" and renders care in good faith to ill or injured passengers during the flight. The wording reads: "*An individual shall not be liable for damages in any action brought in a federal or state court arising from an act or omission of the individual in providing or attempting to provide assistance in the case of an in-flight medical emergency.*"

References

APA Guidelines on Confidentiality.
American Psychiatric Association, Washington D.C., 1987

Appelbaum PS, Grisso T: **Assessing Patients' Capacities to Consent to Treatment**.
NEJM 319:1635-1638, 1988

Appelbaum PS, Jorgenson LM, Sutherland PK: **Sexual Relationships Between Physicians and Patients**.
Arch Intern Med 154:2561-2565, 1994

Appelbaum PS, Grisso T: **Capacities of Hospitalized, Medically Ill Patients to Consent to Treatment**.
Psychosomatics 38:119-125, 1997

Aviation Medical Assistance Act, Public Law 105-170, 1998

Bursztajn HJ, Harding HP, Gutheil TG, et al: **Beyond Cognition: The Role of Disordered Affective States in Impairing Competence to Consent to Treatment**.
Bull Am Acad Psychiatry Law 19:383-388, 1991

Campbell ML: **The Oath: An Investigation of the Injunction Prohibiting Physician-Patient Sexual Relations**.
Perspect Biol Med 32:300-309, 1998

Canterbury v. Spence, 464 F 2d 772 (1972)

Code of Medical Ethics – Current Opinions with Annotations.
American Medical Association, Chicago, 1999

Cruzan v. Director, Missouri Dept of Health. 497 U.S. 261, 1990

Doyal L: **Informed Consent in Medical Research**.
BMJ 314:1107-1111, 1997

Emanuel EJ, Danies ER, Fairclough DL, et al: **The Practice of Euthanasia and Physician-Assisted Suicide in the U.S.: Adherence to Proposed Safeguards and Effects on Physicians**.
JAMA 280:507-513, 1998

Emanuel LL: **Facing Requests for Physician-Assisted Suicide — Toward a Practical Principled Clinical Skill Set**.
JAMA 280:643-647, 1998

Foubister V: **Oregon Doctor Cited for Negligence for Undertreated Pain**.
AMA News 42(45):7, 9, 1999

Gostin LO: **Deciding Life and Death in the Courtroom. From Quinlan to Cruzan, Glucksberg, and Vacco — A Brief History and Analysis of Constitutional Protection of the "Right to Die."**
JAMA 278:1523-1528, 1999

Grisso T, Appelbaum PS: *Assessing Competence to Consent to Treatment.*
Oxford University Press, New York, 1998

Gutheil TG, Bursztajn HJ, Brodsky A: **Malpractice Prevention Through the Sharing of Uncertainty: Informed Consent and the Therapeutic Alliance**.
NEJM 311:49-51, 1984

Gutheil TG, Simon RI: **Between the Chair and the Door: Boundary Issues in the Therapeutic Transition Zon**e.
Harvard Review of Psychiatry 2:336-340, 1995

In re Conroy, 486 A2d 1209 (NJ 1985)

In re Quinlan, 355 A2d 647(NJ), cert. denied, 429 US922 (1976)

Marta M: **Genetic Testing: Do Healthcare Professionals Have a Duty to Tell a Patient's Family Member that They May Be at Risk?**
J Healthcare Risk Management 19:26-38, 1999

McCracken v. Walls, Kaufman 717 A.2d 346(D.C. 1998)

Miller FG, Quill TE, Brody H, et al: **Regulating Physician-Assisted Death**.
NEJM 331:119-123, 1994

Molien v. Kaiser Foundation Hospitals [27 Cal.3d 916] 1980

Natanson v. Kline, 350 P.2d 1093 (Kansas 1960)

Orentlicher D: **Must CPR Be An Issue in Futile Situations?**
AM News 42:9-10, Sept 6, 1999

Pain Relief Promotion Act of 1999. HR 2260

Patient Self-Determination Act of 1990
42 United States Code Sections 1395, 1396

Roush S, Virkhead G, Koo D, et al: **Mandatory Reporting of Diseases and Conditions by Health Care Professionals and Laboratories**.
JAMA 282:164-170, 1999

Rozovsky FA: **When Does "No Mean No" in the Emergency Department?**
The Rozovsky Group, Inc.
www.therozovskygroup.com, reviewed 10/12/99

Scholoendorff v. Society of New York Hospitals, 211 N.Y. 125 (1914)

Searight HR, Campbell DC: **Physician–Patient Sexual Contact: Ethical and Legal Issues and Clinical Guidelines**.
J Fam Pract 36:647-653, 1993

Simon R: **Boundary Violations in Psychotherapy**.
The Mental Health Practitioner and the Law., Ed. Lifson LE and Simon RI.
Harvard Univ Press, Cambridge, 1998

Singer PA, Martin DK, Kelner M: **Quality End-of-Life Care**.
JAMA 281:163-168, 1999

Steinbrook R, Lo B: **Artificial Feeding — Solid Ground, Not a Slippery Slope**.
NEJM 318:286-290, 1988

Tarasoff v. Regents, CA Supr. Ct (1976) 70, 71, 232

Vacco v. Quill, 117 S. Ct 2293, 1997

Washington v. Glucksberg, 117 S. Ct 2258, 1997

4. Odds and Ends

4.1 — Prescribing Issues

4.1.1 — Legibility

In some lawsuits, the signature of the physician is enlarged to fill a five-foot long display. When the jury has the chance to stare at the exhibit for several days, they grow more and more incensed at the illegibility, and decide against the scribbling doctor.

4.1.2 — Drug Name Similarities

Be particularly cautious when you are prescribing one drug that has a similar name to another. This is both a legibility and accuracy issue. A case in point is the similarity in the non-proprietary names of the cardiac drugs *amrinone* and *amiodarone*. The first is a vasodilator with positive inotropic action, the latter an anti-arrhythmic. Confusion between these similar names has so far resulted in 11 medication errors and one death. Authorities proposed a name change for each to avoid further morbidity. An excellent website that will give you updates on medication risk issues and is sponsored by the Institute for Safe Medication Practices is **http:// www.ismp.org**

4.1.3 — Documentation

If it isn't documented – it didn't happen.

4.1.4 — Prescribing and Informed Consent

As with any other evaluation or treatment procedure, prescribing any medication to a patient requires proper informed consent. This involves telling the patient the diagnosis, the risks/benefits of the recommended treatment, the risks/benefits of alternative treatments, and the risks/benefits of receiving no treatment. The legal requirement is that the patient be made aware of her "material risks," or what the reasonable person in the same situation would want to know. This does not mean you need to discuss every possible side-effect listed in the **Physician's Desk Reference** (**PDR**), only the substantial or common ones. Some jurisdictions have determined an actual percentage equating to a material risk. If your jurisdiction defines a material risk as one that occurs at least 1% of the time, then you should tell the patient about the side-effects known to occur with that frequency, as well as the serious side-effects that occur less often.

4.1.5 – Medications Prescribed for a Non-FDA Approved Use

If you are using a drug in a way that is not approved by the FDA (and not noted in the PDR), you must let the patient know this. The lack of official approval does not restrict you from using the medication. Some unapproved medications are the "drug of choice" for treating certain conditions. Before using a medication in a non-approved way, be certain that you have scientific evidence and peer-reviewed articles to back your decision.

4.1.6 – Non-FDA Approved Drugs

A variation on the above theme is the use of a non-approved medication, a situation for which extreme caution is advised. Not uncommonly, medications have been used for years in other countries, but have not received FDA approval (for any of a variety of reasons). While the use of such medications may be well supported by scientific evidence in peer-reviewed journals, it is technically against the law to use them and difficult to defend in a lawsuit. A consent form would be advisable in situations where you intend to proceed with a non-approved medication.

4.1.7 – Exceeding Recommended Doses (In Amount or Frequency)

The PDR is a helpful guide, but if in your opinion (and based on medical evidence), a different dose is appropriate, follow your clinical judgment. This situation is particularly common with the use/amount of pain medication in terminal cancer patients. Ensure proper informed consent is obtained and that your decisions are well documented with regard to how/why you made your decision. Do not avoid giving adequate pain relief for fear of straying from the PDR recommendations — just to be certain to document your rationale.

4.1.8 – Controlled Substances

Be aware of, and abide by, local rules regarding scheduled medications. As an example, Maine physicians now have a new requirement. As of January 1, 2003, all physicians must use a non-duplicable prescription pad when prescribing narcotics. This requirement was implemented in response to a marked increase in the number of deaths related to abuse of narcotics in the preceding two years.

4.1.9 – Prescribing for Yourself or Family Members

Generally, as long as you are not obtaining controlled substances, self-prescribing probably won't get you in trouble, but still isn't a great idea. As long as you are not practicing outside the scope of your training and experience, you usually won't be faulted. If you provide negligent care for your family you aren't likely to be sued, but someone else may report you to your state board of licensure. A legal action could be instituted on behalf of a minor. Remember the time-tested adage — *The doctor who treats herself has a fool for a patient.*

4.1.10 – Knowledge of Allergies

A no-brainer, but errors continue to occur at alarming rates.

4.1.11 – Knowledge of Medications

Do you have a mechanism to ensure that you are aware of all the medications a patient is taking (including nutritional supplements)? A questionnaire that the patient updates at each visit will help make you aware of any changes. This list then behooves you to check for possible interactions. It is estimated that over 50% of patients take some form of non-prescribed medicines or remedies. The PDR publishers offer a volume on dietary supplements. Paperback texts are also available. Many patients are unaware that their "vitamins" are frequently pharmacoactive substances that could be causing, or at least contributing to, their difficulties. These chemicals may interact with prescribed medications and cause complications. For example, a **serotonergic syndrome** can be caused by prescribing an SSRI for a patient whom you did not know was taking St. John's Wort. If the patient doesn't reveal such information, this is one matter, but failing to ask is an entirely different one.

4.1.12 – Monitoring Medications
Regardless of your specialty, many of the medications you use cause side-effects, alter disease processes, and can interact with other medications. You must have some routine for monitoring patients' medications. Again, it is best to brainstorm with your colleagues to find effective solutions. If you have no mechanism in place, you may get a call from the lawyer hired after your patient sustained permanent brain damage from the fall he took (allegedly caused by the orthostatic hypotension that was a prominent side-effect of the medication you just prescribed). Your potential liability soars if:
• You didn't warn the patient about this side-effect
• You didn't arrange a follow-up appointment
• You didn't take a pre-treatment blood pressure reading

4.1.13 – Prescribing For "Ghost" Patients
When you prescribe a medication, you establish a duty to that person. You are clearly safest by never prescribing for "non-patients." If you do, be certain to clearly assess your risks and minimize them. Doctors have lost their medical licenses over "ghost" prescriptions, though this is more likely when controlled substances are involved.

The Internet "Viagra®doc-in-the-box" scenarios are a hot topic. In addition to being liable for negligence (which is difficult to defend if you did not examine the patient — even with the negative cardiac history supplied by the Internet questionnaire), you may also be charged with practicing medicine without a license in the state where the patient resides.

4.1.14 – Prescribing For Other "Not Really My Patient" Patients

This practice can occur in mental health areas where one practitioner provides therapy, another provides social services, and a physician prescribes the medication. The duty here is straightforward. You, the physician, have a duty to the patient for the treatment you provide. If a patient commits suicide with the medication you prescribe, your defense of, "but the therapist didn't tell me he was suicidal" will not play well in court. This is why fragmented situations are fraught with risk. Minimizing risk is accomplished by clear communication and documentation. Ensure that proper informed consent is obtained and the patient is informed about his illness and treatment. You need to assess any potential risks and ensure follow-up. Communicate your actions and findings to everyone else involved in the case.

4.1.15 – Duties to Third Parties

Ensure that you provide a proper warning to patients if you prescribe a medication that may make them drowsy. Your advice should also address not mixing medications with alcohol or other substances (prescription or otherwise). If at all possible, include a family member in the discussion when the patient is elderly or unreliable, as long as the person agrees. In most jurisdictions, you are responsible only for warning a competent person of the potential effects.

4.1.16 – Alternative/Complementary Medicine

Although many practitioners use at least some form of alternative medicine, this is an area of very thin ice when doing a risk management inventory. The question you need to ask yourself is as follows: *"If I am sued for allegedly causing an injury from the use of X (an alternative medicine), would the majority of similarly trained, certified, and experienced providers be able to testify that what I did upheld the standard of care?"*

If not, be wary — even if you believe that what you are doing is innocuous and can "cause no harm." A substance that by itself is not harmful can give rise to a variety of legal claims. For example, remember that any non-consensual touching constitutes battery (an intentional tort). Again, you should be careful to have written informed consent for alternative treatments, even if it involves something non-invasive.

The use of herbal medicines and nutritional supplements follows the same rationale. If you are practicing family medicine in Germany, where all doctors are trained in alternative and herbal medicines, you will be practicing at the standard of care. If you are doing the same thing in Billings, MT, or Augusta, GA, the outcome may be very different.

Check your malpractice insurance policy! In one malpractice case, the physician was sued for negligence after an injury was found to be related to the use of an alternative medicine. His insurance company refused to pay for the damages because the policy had a clause excluding coverage for the use of any drug not approved by the FDA. The doctor argued that the substance used was not a drug. The courts disagreed. The definition of a drug was based on the doctor's intent, rather than on the physical composition of the substance. In another case, a physician's medical license was revoked because he prescribed alternative medicines even though there was no evidence that an injury was caused by this treatment. The revocation was based on the state statute in that the doctor "failed to conform to the standards of acceptable and prevailing medical practice." If you do choose to use alternative/complementary medicine, you must ensure that patients are aware of any available conventional treatment for their illnesses and that they are agreeing to forgo conventional treatments.

4.2 – Conflicts of Interest

Potential conflicts of interest were discussed in the Boundary Issues section. For psychiatrists, the mantra for staying clear of conflicts of interest is *"once a patient, always a patient."* Physicians from all areas of medicine would be well served by adhering to this principle. You will avoid potential conflicts of interest if you ensure that you do not put yourself in a position to gain financially or personally from your relationship with a patient (current or former). This means no stock tips, no business partnerships, and no close friendships. The intrinsic satisfaction you get from providing quality medical care is all the benefit you can safely get (and should need) from dealing with patients. Period.

4.2.1 – The Sale of Products In Your Office

A recent debate within the AMA centered on the practice of selling medical products from professional offices. The "pro" argument for this practice is that the patient should have the chance to purchase the "best" products for their various conditions. By offering these products to the patient in your office, you are theoretically helping. If you sell the product at cost (that is, no profit), no potential conflict of interest exists. The "con" argument is that patients may feel coerced into purchasing these products from their physicians. This (potential) sense of coercion results from the imbalance of power, control, and authority, which is inherent in the doctor-patient relationship. This issue is particularly important if you stand to profit from patients' purchases. This issue is no different than referring patients to facilities where you have a financial interest for medical tests. Rather than find a way to rationalize this activity, your safest option is to avoid putting yourself in an ethically compromised position.

☞ Caveat

To be on the ethical high ground, you need to tell patients whenever you stand to gain something (monetarily or otherwise) from decisions involving their care.

The current guidelines from the AMA Council on Ethical and Judicial Affairs reiterate the above recommendations. If you decide to sell products in your office, the following requirements should be met:
- No profit is to be made from selling these items
- No semblance of coercion should enter the process
- Full disclosure of the financial incentives must be made

4.2.2 – Gifts from Pharmaceutical Companies

This continues to be a hot topic because of the potential influence on physicians' prescribing practices. A further concern is that the cost of these initiatives is passed onto patients. Pharmaceutical companies don't spend millions of dollars yearly on gifts out of sheer gratitude. The more that a pharmaceutical company stands to gain from any gift or service, the more stringent you need to be in accepting its offers. Further, the more authority you have in an organization, the greater is the potential for "undue influence" over your decisions. The safest practice for medical directors and **Vice-Presidents of Medical Affairs** (**VPMA**) is to accept no gift worth more than $5.

The AMA Council on Ethical and Judicial Affairs developed guidelines for this area. Their recommendation is that gifts must be of modest value (absolutely under $100), and provide some benefit to patients. Many organizations have policies that are much more conservative. For example, an organization might dictate that no gift from an industry can be accepted if its value is greater than $20, with a limit of $50 per year. The intent of this restriction is to avoid any influence on the purchaser/prescriber and to remove any perception of impropriety. These limitations also apply to other industries, such as medical supply companies, equipment suppliers, etc.

There is widespread agreement that inexpensive items that may benefit patients are acceptable (e.g. pens, note pads, patient information kits, some textbooks, etc.).

☞ Caveat

A conflict of interest is *not* an ethical dilemma. A **conflict of interest** places one set of values over another (i.e. your interests over the patient's). An **ethical dilemma** is one that has two competing values, each of which are in the best interests of patients. Ethical dilemmas may involve end of life issues, civil commitment, or issues that may pit the best interests of one patient against the best interests of another (e.g. transplant organ allocation).

4.3 – Technology

The advances made over the past few decades have been tremendous, both in number and scope. As with most advances, problems also arise, necessitating an awareness of the pitfalls. Some examples follow.

4.3.1 – Telemedicine

Telemedicine is defined as the practice of medicine across distance through the use of telecommunication and interactive video technology. There has been a huge increase in the number of sites using this technology (1,750 in 1993 to 18,766 in 1996). The primary concerns raised about telemedicine are as follows:

1. Who has the duty? There is no simple answer, nor has this been established by case law. Arguments can be made both ways. On one hand, the doctor who provides the care has the duty to the patient. The consulting physician offers advice that the primary doctor can take or leave. On the other hand, if a physician reviews the chart, looks at X-rays, "sees" the patient, provides a consult note, and is paid for this service, many courts would argue that the tele-consultant has indeed established a doctor-patient relationship.

2. What is the standard of care? Thus far, there are limited recommendations on standards for physicians to follow in telemedicine cases. The American College of Radiology was the first to establish such standards. Other specialty societies have been strongly encouraged to follow suit.

3. What about licensure? State statutes vary greatly in their wording regarding what constitutes the practice of medicine, and whether they have agreements with other states or special clauses. Even if a tele-consultant is not found liable for malpractice in a case, she can face both civil and criminal penalties for practicing medicine without a license in many states. Of note, Alabama has one of the most advanced statutes in this regard and offers reciprocity to physicians for the provision of telemedicine services if they are licensed elsewhere.

The licensure issues in telemedicine are similar to those faced by health plan "advice nurses," toll-free numbers for medical advice, and physician-reviewers for managed care plans. Also be aware of any HIPAA issues regarding your use of telemedicine.

4.4 — Oops!

What do you do if you've done everything right (or even if you haven't) and something unforeseen happens? Frequently, the issue involves an unfavorable or unexpected outcome. A recommended approach (with some caveats) is to empathize with the patient's suffering and express your concern. This is like an apology, but done in a "safer" way. Although the insurance company/risk manager/lawyer will tell you not to speak with the patient or family when something goes wrong, this may well not be good advice.

☞ Caveat

"It is not what a lawyer tells me I may do; but what humanity, reason, and justice tell me I ought to do."
     Edmund Burke

Most physicians fear that if they tell a patient they're "sorry," it will be an acknowledgement of wrongdoing. While perhaps you shouldn't bare your soul and make profuse apologies. You can, at the very least, acknowledge the patient's suffering.

If the injury is minor, such as an unpleasant side-effect of a medication you prescribed, you can say something like *"I'm sorry you are so nauseated. We discussed the possibility of this happening but I'm sorry you feel so badly. Let's wait until you feel a little better, and then we'll talk about the other choices we discussed."*

If a more serious, unfavorable outcome occurs, you do not need to go into detail, but you can show the same concern that you would demonstrate if you weren't afraid of being sued. You might say something like *"I understand how badly you feel,"* or *"I wanted to check to see if you needed anything."* If pressed with questions about what happened, tell the person you will get back to her. You may not avoid a lawsuit, but by showing compassion, you will demonstrate that you are not an uncaring monster. Too many physicians have refused to speak with their patients following unfavorable outcomes. In many cases, it is this apparent lack of compassion (or arrogance) that incites the patient to take legal action.

Massachusetts started the trend in 1986 with a fantastic law called the **Admissibility of Benevolent Statements, Writings or Gestures Relating to Accident Victims**. This is better known as the forward-thinking **Apology Statute**. This law reads, *"Statements, writings, or benevolent gestures expressing sympathy or a general sense of benevolence relating to the pain, suffering or death of a person involved in an accident, and made to such person or to the family of such person, shall be inadmissible as evidence of an admission of liability in a civil action."*

In the above paragraph, an **accident** is defined as "an occurrence resulting in injury or death to one or more persons which is not the result of willful action by a party." **Benevolent gestures** are "actions which convey a sense of compassion or commiseration emanating from humane impulses." While it is sad to have to legislate compassion for human suffering, this is one of the most eloquent statutes ever passed. It allows physicians to do what comes naturally — provide for the relief of human suffering. Currently three other states (TX, CA, and FL) have a similar statute, and two (NH and VT) have case law that offers a similar protection. Several other states have legislation underway or proposed. Ask your state medical association about the presence/status of a nondisclosure statute.

References

Appelbaum PS: **General Guidelines for Psychiatrists who Prescribe Medication for Patients Treated by Non-Medical Therapists**.
Hospital and Community Psychiatry 42:281-282, 1991

Bursztajn HJ, Brodsky A: **A New Resource for Managing Malpractice Risks in Managed Care**.
Arch Intern Med 156:2057-2063, 1996
General Laws of Massachusetts, Chapter 233: Section 23D (1986)

Grinfield MJ: **Telemedicine Law Struggles to Keep Up With Technology**.
Psychiatric Times Aug 1999:20-21

Gutheil TG, Gabbard GO: **The Concept of Boundaries in Clinical Practice: Theoretical and Risk Management Dimensions**. *Am J Psych* 150:188-196, 1993

Hilliard J: **Pitfalls of Prescribing Medications**. *The Mental Health Pract.and the Law*. Harvard University Press, Boston, 1998

Hodge JG, Gostin LO, Jacobson PD: **Legal Issues Concerning Electronic Health Information**. *JAMA* 282:1466-1471, 1999

Kaar JF: **Legal Challenges to the Implementation of Telehealth Within the United States and Internationally**. *Legal Medicine* 98:32, 1998

Madden J: **What Are The Limits for Drug Company Gifts?** *Am Med News* 42:10, 9/6/99

Mitka M: **What's In A (Drug) Name? Plenty!** *JAMA* 282:1409, 1999

Morreim EH: **Conflicts of Interest: Profits and Problems in Physician Referrals**. *JAMA* 262:390-394, 1989

Rodwin MA: **Physicians Conflict of Interest: The Limitations of Disclosure**. *NEJM* 321:1405, 1989

Shotwell LF: **Telemedicine and Malpractice: Old Liabilities and New Risks**. Arent Fox Newsletter Vol 1, www. arentfox.com newsletter, accessed 12/5/99

Studdert DM, Eisenberg DM, Curto DA et al: **Medical Malpractice Implications of Alternative Medicine**. *JAMA* 280:1610-1615, 1998

Thomson DF: **Understanding Financial Conflicts of Interest**. *NEJM* 329:573-576, 1993

5. Limiting Liability

"A long habit of not thinking a thing wrong, gives it a superficial appearance of being right."

Thomas Paine, *Common Sense*

5.1– Patient Safety

Since the publication of the Institute of Medicine report, *To Err is Human*, the focus of many healthcare oversight bodies has been directed to the issues of patient safety. Much of this has been for the benefit of improving healthcare processes and decreasing the risk of harm to our patients. Several helpful websites addressing patient safety are:

http://www.medicalerrors.ca/institutes.html
http://www.ahrq.gov — Agency for Healthcare Research and Quality
http://www.npsf.org — National Patient Safety Foundation
http://www.ismp.org — Institute for Safe Medication Practices
http://www.jcaho.org — Joint Commission for the Accreditation of Health Care Organizations

The organizations involved in the improvement of patient safety emphasize that medical error is about systems and processes, not about individuals. Contrary to the quality assurance (QA) programs of the past, the focus is not on placing blame, but rather looking at root causes and institutionalizing process improvements to ensure a safer healthcare system. These concepts are nicely summarized in an article from the National Patient Safety Foundation website listed above.

5.1.1 – The ABCs of Patient Safety

Accountability is not always about a person.
Blame hides the truth about error.
Cultures must change.

5.2 – Communication

Developing superior communication skills is crucial for physicians who want to improve their "art of medicine" abilities and take effective steps in limiting their legal liability.

5.2.2 – Factoids on Communication

- A finding frequently quoted in training seminars is that during routine patient visits, doctors interrupted and redirected their patients within 18 seconds. This immediately sets the stage for patients to feel ignored and patronized.
- Another study demonstrated that although physicians solicited their patients' concerns in 75% of the cases, patients were able to complete their initial statements only 28% of the time, and were redirected after only 23 seconds. When patients were allowed to complete their full communication, they needed on average only 6 additional seconds!
- Thirty-five percent of the patients who were redirected during interviews raised additional concerns at the end of the evaluation, compared to only 15% of the patients who were able to complete their initial statements.
- In a survey of physicians who had not been the subject of a lawsuit, the majority credited rapport, good communication, and compassion for patients as the reasons they had been able to stay out of court. Only 14% credited their good medical skills.

Communication can be enhanced without necessarily spending more time with patients. This is accomplished by maximizing the efficiency of their visits.

5.3 – Patients Who Have Chronic Diseases

A key recommendation is to tell patients to keep a list of their questions. It can be helpful to tell them ahead of time that you may not have the chance to discuss all of their concerns, but you are interested in knowing what bothers them the most. By simply asking about their principal concerns, you convey a strong sense of genuinely caring for your patients' welfare.

5.3.1 – Initial Evaluations

It can be very helpful to develop a questionnaire that centers on your area of expertise, but that also covers peripheral areas. Examples of the latter are: domestic abuse, tobacco use (all forms), alcohol use, allergies, and a list of all medications, including vitamins, nutritional supplements, herbal medicines, etc. An appropriately trained assistant can review the questionnaire, clarify the information provided, and begin health promotion and education (e.g. tobacco cessation). Patients could then watch videotapes geared towards their particular education needs — all while waiting to see you.

One of the main reasons patients dislike visiting physicians is that they are kept waiting without an explanation. A helpful guideline is the "Twenty Minute Rule." This involves having a staff member inform patients about the reason for any delay, and the approximate additional wait within 20 minutes of the scheduled appointment. An apology for the delay goes a long way towards ensuring patient satisfaction. If delays aren't acknowledged, patients feel that their time is not considered to be valuable.

Consider the situation where someone who is an established patient of your practice leaves because he was not seen in a timely fashion. If a follow-up appointment is not arranged, and something happens because he wasn't assessed, you may well be liable even though it was the patient who left. This is based on your duty to, and abandonment of, the patient.

If that same patient storms out the door on several occasions and is rude to your staff, it may well be time to arrange for someone else to take over that person's care using the stepwise approach noted in the abandonment section (Section 3.17). Enhancing communication at the team level is also important. Many organizations are learning tools from other high risk industries that have addressed safety. One example is that of Crew Resource Management from aviation. There are excellent training courses that have been adapted to medicine.

5.4 — Documentation

Good documentation is crucial to good patient care. Even a physician with total recall for every patient's diagnosis, list of medications, lab values, dates of preventive actions, etc. can still get run over by a truck. Good charting practices allow everyone involved in the patient's care to share information, which enhances medical decision-making.

There are many state laws governing medical documentation. If your organization is assessed by the Joint Commission for Health Care Organizations, or the National Committee for Quality Assurance, medical record documentation is a major focus. Unfortunately, for many physicians, writing in the medical record takes a back seat to other patient care priorities.

☞ Modified Nike® Caveat

Just do it, but simply.

There are many excellent references that provide guidelines for improving documentation. The process of improving documentation begins with your own critical review. Do your notes show that you discussed the diagnosis? Can your records provide evidence that informed consent was obtained for any treatment or procedure? Was the rationale for ongoing treatment explained, as well as the necessity for follow-up visits?

Ensure that your staff documents their interactions with patients as well. Medical notes do not need to be lengthy, they just need to cover the essentials.

Stocking a complete set of patient education handouts is a great way of doing the most with a limited amount of time. You or your nurse can review the handout with the patient and answer any questions. Record these questions, and indicate that they were reviewed. If you use the same handouts consistently, you don't need to write a novel for each diagnosis, just document that you have provided and reviewed the handout with the patient.

5.5 – Corrections to Medical Records

5.5.1 – Changes Should "Stand Alone"

Anyone reviewing the medical record should be able to easily tell when, why, and who made any changes. Many physicians put a line through the original entry, and then initial and date the alteration. However, this doesn't satisfy the "stand alone" requirement. As an example, let's say you write an entry in another patient's chart. Put an 'X' through your note and write in the margin "Entry in wrong record," and then initial and date it. In the correct record, write a note stating "Entry for such-and-such date written in wrong record."

5.5.2 – Do Not Obliterate Entries

If the record is ever used in litigation, it will look like you did something wrong and were trying to hide this fact, even if it was something innocuous. A good lawyer will enlarge an obliterated entry to a disquieting four-foot by six-foot size and make it an exhibit. When jurors are bored by listening to medical testimony, their gaze will be drawn to this display.

Furthermore, the technology available today to date documents, papers, and inks is quite powerful. Do not try to "fix" a record if you are concerned about a lawsuit or have received a subpoena. Be honest. If there is proof that you intentionally tried to change a record to avoid blame, the lawsuit may now enter the realm of intentional tort. If there is evidence that a physician participated in a cover-up of some sort, the usual statute of limitations for negligence may not apply. Juries want to find for the defendant physician, and will accept honest mistakes. But they don't like liars.

5.5.3 – An Example of a Correction to a Medical Record
Original Note
3/3/03: Jane Doe is a 37-year-old male with IDDM and erectile dysfunction. Viagra® has been ineffective and she has now become depressed with and developed suicidal ideation because of this condition, with concurrent marital discord. Her depression is believed to be secondary to her medical condition. No imminent risk for self harm, either plan or intent, was elicited. Will follow closely.

Wrong Method of Correction
~~3/3/03: Jane Doe is a 37-year-old male with IDDM and erectile dysfunction. Viagra® has been ineffective and she has now become depressed with and developed suicidal ideation because of this condition, with concurrent marital discord. Her depression is believed to be secondary to her medical condition. No imminent risk for self harm, either plan or intent, was elicited.~~
Will follow closely.

This method of correction leaves no clue as to what was written or what the problem was. This entry could be disastrous if it is used as evidence in a medical malpractice case. Striking out an entry makes it look like a physician is trying to hide what was written, not simply correcting an erroneous entry.

Right Method of Correction

This entry "stands alone," it can still be read and there is a dated entry indicating the error.

3/3/03: ~~Jane Doe is a 37-year-old male with IDDM and erectile dysfunction. Viagra® has been ineffective and she has now become depressed with and developed suicidal ideation because of this condition, with concurrent marital discord. Her depression is believed to be secondary to her medical condition. No imminent risk for self harm, either plan or intent, was elicited. Will follow closely.~~

(3/10/03: The above entry is incorrect — it was written in the wrong chart. The correct entry was for John Doe on that date. DJW-F.)

5.5.4 – Write Legibly

Poor handwriting can be the cause of a court decision against you. Physicians have a duty to write so those involved in a patient's care can read what has been said. Illegible progress notes can be a problem, but the greatest legal risk comes from unreadable treatment orders or prescriptions. If the proverbial "reasonable person" cannot decipher your hieroglyphics, it is quite likely that you will be hung out to dry. Poor penmanship can be seen as stemming from arrogance, and those around you are subsequently less likely to be there to help you in the hundreds of subtle ways that can make your job easier.

5.5.5 – Keep Personal Opinions about the Care Provided by Others Out of the Medical Record

Any concern you have about the care rendered to Mrs. Smithereen by another member of the treatment team should be discussed with that person and addressed through your organization's risk management process. The medical record is a legal document and may be fully discoverable in court. Quality assurance/risk management documents are generally not discoverable, although in some jurisdictions judges may be allowed to review this information. If you are a consultant and have found that the patient's primary physician has prescribed a medication that you do not recommend, you can of course record this in your recommendations, and can add "Will discuss choice of meds with Dr. Lecter."

☞ **Caveat**

If you make disparaging comments of any nature in the medical record, in addition to being inappropriate, you may well have freely provided full documentation in a defamation suit – against you!

5.5.6 – Make Certain Your Statements Aren't Ambiguous

Here are some gems. These bloopers have been collected from several sources, and are allegedly from actual medical records:

- "Patient evaluated by social worker found to be psychotic."
- "The patient refused an autopsy."
- "Patient had waffles for breakfast and anorexia for lunch."
- "She is numb from her toes down."
- "On the 2nd day the knee was better and on the 3rd day it disappeared completely."
- "Patient was alert and unresponsive."
- "The patient has been depressed ever since she began seeing me in 1993."
- "Rectal exam revealed a normal size thyroid."
- "Testicles are missing on this woman."
- "Patient has two teenage children but no other abnormalities."
- "Large brown stool ambulating in hall."
- "I saw your patient today who is still under our car for physical therapy."
- "She stated she has been constipated for most of her life, until she got a divorce."
- "If it weren't for the fact the patient is dead, I would say he was in perfect health."
- "Discharge status — alive but without permission."

5.5.7 – Duration of Custody for Medical Records

Check your state laws to determine how long you need to keep medical records. The state will also indicate what should occur when you retire or die. If you conduct psychotherapy or provide perinatal care, it is prudent to keep your records forever (or at least a summary of them). You must have some provision in your will for who will become the guardian of your records.

5.6 — Consultations

Requesting consultations from other physicians, on either a formal or informal basis, ensures that patients receive an appropriate level of care. Every state requires physicians to practice within their areas of expertise and to provide a level of care that a similarly trained and experienced colleague would provide. As Harry Callahan (of *Dirty Harry* fame) wisely said, "A man's gotta know his limitations." This applies even more so to physicians. The majority of medical practitioners are comfortable knowing when to ask for help or a second opinion. Unfortunately, those who don't ask for assistance are often the ones who need it the most.

A valuable tool in your armamentarium of good patient care (and an asset in minimizing risk) is the informal or "curbside" consult. This term refers to a communication between colleagues where a clinical problem is succinctly presented and advice is sought for a specific point or two. Curbside consults are underused, and a win-win proposition. Many physicians are hesitant to offer curbside opinions because of their legal liability. This is largely an unfounded concern. A worst-case scenario is as follows:

Dr. Smith is treating Mrs. Finicky, and informally consults Dr. Jones about her care. Dr. Smith's case presentation begins as follows "This is a 45-year-old woman with a two month history of. . ." No name is given, and Dr. Jones never sees the patient. Following a discussion about possible diagnostic and treatment alternatives, Dr. Smith writes in the chart "Case discussed with Dr. Jones."

If Mrs. Finicky sues following an unfavorable outcome, it is likely that everyone whose name is noted in the medical record will be named in the lawsuit. When Dr. Jones is asked about the case, either in an initial investigation or during a deposition, the conversation with the lawyer will likely follow something along these lines:

Lawyer: "Dr. Jones, did you evaluate Mrs. Finicky as a consultant for Dr. Smith?"
Dr. Jones: "No, I did not."

Lawyer: "But Dr. Jones, your name is in the medical record."

Dr. Jones: "Yes, Dr. Smith and I may have discussed the case."

Lawyer: "Dr. Jones, are you saying you didn't personally examine Mrs. Finicky?"

Dr. Jones: "That is correct. I have never examined or evaluated Mrs. Finicky. Dr. Smith may have discussed her case with me. We frequently discuss our cases with each other."

Lawyer: "Why would you do that?"

Dr. Jones: "We discuss cases in order to get the opinion of another practitioner. We believe that this improves the quality of the patient care in our practices."

Juries love testimony like this. It goes a long way towards demonstrating that you value the opinions of others, and that you are not one of those physicians who is seen as arrogantly flapping around in *status narcissisticus*. (This wonderful visual image was coined by Dr. Thomas Gutheil and used during his presentations).

The only possible problem with the curbside consult is that if your colleague gives you bad advice, and you take it, you are liable, not your casually consulted colleague. Unless Dr. Smith formally requests a consultation and Dr. Jones evaluates Mrs. Finicky (or in some jurisdictions just her medical record), duty has not been established.

☞ **Caveat**

Curbside consultations are not a replacement for a formal evaluation by a specialist. Curbside consults are usually requested by physicians who would not otherwise consider requesting a formal consult or could not justify it in a capitated/managed care setting. If you request a curbside consult, or get asked about one, make it clear that this is what is being sought. In order to have established duty, either the patient must be interviewed/examined or the chart reviewed (depending on state statutes). Liability for the requesting physician/consultee is established as follows: if the consultee wholeheartedly implements the consultant's suggestions, and a similarly trained and experienced physician would not have, the consultee is responsible for what happens to the patient as a result of a curbside consultation. This is also true in formal consultations, but the liability would be shared because *both* physicians have the duty in formal consults.

5.7 — Process Issues

Processes are all of the "things" that you, your staff, or your organization does which affect or involve the patient, not just the actual evaluation and treatment. Processes are generally system issues, and even the smallest practice should have some mechanism to identify the areas that are "high risk/high volume" for your specific area of practice. Some of these issues fall into either the Bad Feeling/Bad Outcome part of the liability equation. Suggestions for limiting your liability due to administrative processes are as follows:

- Have a system in place to ensure that all ordered tests (lab, X-ray, etc.) are reported, and that you have a clearly defined system for feedback and follow-up
- Conduct an annual brainstorming session with your staff to review the "soup to nuts" processes that affect your practice (e.g. ease of making appointments, directions to your office, parking, availability of childcare facilities, patient rights and responsibilities visibly posted, cleanliness of bathroom, correction of billing errors, etc.)
- Have a system in place where staff, patients, and visitors can provide you with feedback (anonymously if they choose) on anything that can be improved

When others know that you are interested in their ideas, it goes a long way to ensuring their trust. If at all possible, implement some of the suggestions you are given as soon as possible. Train your staff to be able to handle patient complaints and to know when to seek assistance from someone up the chain.

References

Beckman HB, Markakis KM, Suchman AL et al: **The Doctor-Patient Relationship and Malpractice: Lessons From Plaintiff Depositions**.
Arch Intern Med 154:1365-1370, 1994

Berner M: Write Smarter, Not Longer.
The Mental Health Practitioner and the Law.
Ed. Lifson LE and Simon RI.
Harvard Univ Press, Cambridge, 1998

Crane M: **Malpractice Survey**. *Medical Economics* 26 July 1999

Documentation Guidelines for Evaluation and Management Services.
Medicare B Newsletter, Nov 1994

Haas D, Zipperer L: **The ABC's of Patient Safety**. www.npsf.org.
Accessed 1/13/2003

Kohn LT, Corrigan JM, et. al: **To Err is Human: Building a Safer Health System**.
Institute of Medicine, The National Academies Press, 2000

Levinson W, Roter DL, Mullooly JP et al: **Physician-Patient Communication: The Relationship With Malpractice Claims Arising From Primary Care Physicians and Surgeons**.
JAMA 277:553-559, 1997

Marvel MK, Epstein RM, Flowers K et. al: **Soliciting the Patient's Agenda — Have We Improved?**
JAMA 281:283-287, 1999

22 Commandments for a Legally Sound Practice

I. Practice within the scope of your training, experience, and privileging.

II. Never place your needs above those of your patients.

III. Ensure proper informed consent is obtained and that you disclose all treatment options.

IV. Avoid all personal relationships with your patients.

V. Make every attempt to listen to your patients.

VI. Try hard to empathize, even with the unlikable.

VII. Never promise a result.

VIII. Demonstrate compassion in the face of suffering.

IX. Document (legibly and concisely) what you have done.

X. Ensure proper professional liability coverage (which includes coverage for administrative responsibilities).

XI. Consult with legal counsel sooner rather than later.

XII. Demonstrate humility toward patients and staff (even if it is not your nature to do so).

XIII. Become aware of your state laws and local policies.

XIV. Document the reasons for your decision if it deviates from established guidelines or requirements.

XV. Seek assistance when your opinion differs from that of your patient.

XVI. Respect the right of your patient to refuse your recommended treatment.

XVII. Do not ask your own patients to participate in your research (and if you must, obtain impeccable informed consent).

XVIII. Recognize that you have assumed a duty for anyone to whom you have provided medical advice.

XIX. Ensure that your patients have the capacity to consent to your treatments.

XX. Do not participate in physician–assisted suicide unless you reside in Oregon.

XXI. Do no disclose information about your patients unless they request you to do so, or unless you are legally ordered to do so.

XXII. Place the safety of your patients above all else.

Index

A

Abandonment 94
Advance Directives 84
Against Medical Advice (**AMA**) 69-70
Alternative Dispute Resolution (**ADR**) 25
Alternative Medicine 104
American Medical Association (**AMA**) 8
Americans with Disabilities Act (**ADA**) 44-46
Anti-dumping Law 42
Anti-kickback Statute 39-40
Autonomy 8

B

Beneficence 8
Benevolent Gestures 110
Bragdon v. Abbott 45
Boundary Crossings 88-90
Boundary Issues 88-93
Boundary Violations 90-93

C

Capacity 60
Capacity to Make Medical
    Decisions 59-64
    Example 61
    Elements 62-64
Clinical Practice Guidelines 29
Commandments for a Legally Sound
    Practice 124-125
Communication 113
Competence 60
Competence to Make Medical
    Decisions 59-64
    Example 61
    Elements 62-64
Confidentiality 72
    Exceptions 74
Conflicts of Interest 105-107
Consultations 120

Contributory Negligence 25
Controlled Substances 102

D

Damage 16, 19
Dereliction 16
Department of Health and Human
    Services (**DHHS**) 65
Direct Causation 16, 18
Documentation 57-9, 115-16
    See also Medical Records
Dual Agency 75
Dual Relationships 94
Duty 16, 18
    to third parties 75
Duty to Protect 75
Duty to Warn 75

E

Economic Informed Consent 67
Emancipated Minor 77
Emergency Medical Treatment and
    Active Labor Act of 1986
    (**EMTALA**) 42-43
End of Life Issues 81-84
Equal Employment Opportunity
    Commission (**EEOC**) 47-48
Ethics 7, 107
Ethics in Patient Referral Act 40

F

False Imprisonment 71-72
Federal Register 47
Food and Drug Administration (**FDA**) 101

G

Ghost Patients 103
Ghost Surgery 54
Good Samaritan Laws 96

H

Health Insurance Portability and
    Accountability Act of 1996
    (**HIPAA**) 36-38

Hospice   87–88

I

Informed Consent   50–59
    Development   52–54
    Documenting   57
    Economic   67
    Example   58
    Exceptions   55
    Obtaining   51–52
    Prescribing Medication
        100–101
Institutional Ethics Committees (**IEC**)
    86

L

Law   7
    Source of   14–16

M

Materiality of Information Standard
    53
Medical Records   116–120
    Corrections   116–118
Mini-Mental State Exam (**MMSE**)
    61
Minors   66–68, 77–78

N

National Institute of Mental Health
    (**NIMH**)   65
National Practitioner Data Bank
    (**NPDB**)
    29
Nonmalfeasance   8
Nuisance Lawsuits   30

O

Occupational, Safety, and Health
    Administration (**OSHA**)
    46
Office for Protection for Research
    Risks (**OPRR**)   65

P

Patient Safety   112
Physician Extender   28
Physician–Assisted Suicide
    85–86

Physician's Desk Reference (**PDR**)
    100, 101
Prescribing Issues   100–105
Privilege   79
Process Issues   122
Professional Liability Insurance
    48

Q

Qui Tam   38–39

R

Reasonable Medical Practitioner
    Standard   53
Regulatory Agencies   34–39, 41–42
Release of Medical Information
    76–77
Repondeat Superior   28
Res Ipsa Loquitor   26
Research   65–66
Right to Die   81
Right to Refuse Treatment
    68

S

Self-Determination   59
Stabilization   43
Standard of Care   20–24
Standard of Proof   17–18
Standby   93
Stark I and II Laws   40
Statute of Limitations   25
Subpoenas   79–81

T

Tarasoff Decisions   75
Therapeutic Privilege   56
Therapeutic Waiver   56
Third Parties
    Duties to   79, 104
    Release of Information
    76–77
    Liability   78
Torts   30–33
    Intentional   16, 30
    Unintentional   16, 30

V

Vicarious Liability   26, 27

The Author

Dr. Wear-Finkle is a forensic and aerospace psychiatrist with a clinical and consulting practice in Brunswick, Maine. She is board certified in adult and forensic psychiatry, and is an adjunct assistant professor at the Uniformed Services University of the Health Sciences in Bethesda, Maryland. She completed residency training in internal medicine, practiced in both psychiatry and operational medicine, and has management experience as chief operating officer for an ambulatory care clinic. Dr. Wear-Finkle has been involved in policy development and healthcare planning. She has served as a chief of the medical staff for several organizations, a risk manager, and as a consultant to NASA.

The Artist

Brian Chapman is a resident of Oakville, Ontario, Canada. He was born in Sussex, England and moved to Canada in 1957. Brian was formerly a Creative Director at Mediacom. He continues to freelance and is versatile in a wide range of media. He is a master of the caricature, and his talents are constantly in demand.

Rapid Psychler Press

In addition to textbooks, Rapid Psychler Press specializes in producing 35mm slides, overhead transparencies, and digital images for presentations.